FLORIDA STATE
UNIVERSITY LIBRARIES

MAR 7 1996

TALLAHASSEE, FLORIDA

The Modern Jewish Experience

The Modern Jewish Experience

Advisory Editor

Moses Rischin

Editorial Board

Arthur A. Goren

Irving Howe

MY PORTION

(An Autobiography)

REBEKAH KOHUT

ARNO PRESS

A New York Times Company

New York / 1975

HQ
1413
K6
A37
1975

Reprint Edition 1975 by Arno Press Inc.

Reprinted from a copy in
The Newark Public Library

THE MODERN JEWISH EXPERIENCE
ISBN for complete set: 0-405-06690-2
See last pages of this volume for titles.

Manufactured in the United States of America

Library of Congress Cataloging in Publication Data

Kohut, Rebekah Bettelheim, 1864-1951.
  My portion.

  (The Modern Jewish experience)
  Reprint of the 1925 ed. published by T. Seltzer, New York.
  1. Kohut, Rebekah Bettelheim, 1864-1951. I. Title.
II. Series.
HQ1413.K6A37   1975   296'.092'4 B   74-27995
ISBN 0-405-06722-4

My Portion

REBEKAH KOHUT

MY PORTION

(An Autobiography)

Introduction by
HENRIETTA SZOLD

NEW YORK
THOMAS SELTZER
1925

Copyright, 1925, by
THOMAS SELTZER, INC.

All Rights Reserved

PRINTED IN THE UNITED STATES OF AMERICA

To my friend
ALBERT A. BERG, M. D.
Healer and Humanitarian

Contents

CHAPTER		PAGE
	INTRODUCTION	ix
I	HUNGARY	3
II	RICHMOND	16
III	WESTWARD WE GO	35
IV	GROWING PAINS	49
V	SPIRITUAL TRIALS	63
VI	NEW YORK	87
VII	"SO GREAT A DECISION"	103
VIII	MARRIAGE	118
IX	EUROPE	134
X	LUCK'S PERSECUTIONS	154
XI	THE MEMORIAL LIGHT	166
XII	BEYOND	183
XIII	EMERGENCE OF THE JEWESS	192
XIV	AFFLUENCE	206
XV	RIVERDALE	237
XVI	SOCIAL WORK	254
XVII	OVERSEAS ACTIVITIES	265
XVIII	MY PORTION	285

INTRODUCTION

Some of the readers of Mrs. Kohut's memoirs will recall the time when it was a truism that Jewish literature is singularly wanting in personal reminiscences. They will remember that a generation ago the publication of Glückel von Hameln's Diary was little short of a sensational event. For over a hundred and fifty years the highly significant historical material it contained had lain hidden in the obscurity of a manuscript buried in family archives. Yet its actual, scientific value was for the first moment eclipsed by the interest it aroused through the fact that an autobiographical record had been added to the meagre Jewish literature of its kind, and the interest was further deepened by the circumstance that it was the autobiography of a woman.

That Jewish literature should be deficient in personal material lay in the nature of Jewish life as it was perforce constituted. In the overwhelming sum of Jewish communal woe and communal aspiration, the individual sank out of sight. His personal desires, trials, and successes were frail straws rapidly swirled out of sight on the stream of community life. From the Jewish point of view the public weal was better served by reticence than by self-expression. In the moving Jewish drama, the chorus alone was vocal. Only at critical times it would happen that the recluse scholar disengaged himself from the background as a speaking character, to admonish in the face of spiritual backsliding or encourage in the face of danger; or the man of affairs was forced into leadership, to save his brethren by his wealth or his resourceful wit, when expulsion or massacre threatened. These two outstanding figures were not tempted to self-revelation. The scholar's work spoke for him; the intercessor's was too delicate to court publicity. They remained silent, and by their silence emphasized the relation of the individual to the commuity and of the community to the individual.

The passing of the Ghetto, the enforced and the self-imposed, marked a change in this mutual relation. The Jew out in the large world felt impelled to reveal himself to his community, no longer his sole environment. The revelation was the pledge of his continued loyalty. It indicated his new type of usefulness to it. No less he felt the need of making himself known to his associates at whose side he trod the broad walks of life. He had leaped over barriers and triumphed over obstacles. He felt that his way of entering what had been alien surroundings was both interesting and instructive. His conquests were a tribute to the order under which he and his fellow-workers lived. His activities were a contribution

Introduction

to the civic advance towards social harmony, whether viewed from the Jewish side or the world's.

And who in his progress has more obstacles to overcome than the immigrant, which the Jew too often is for the good of his spiritual oneness? And if the immigrant is a woman to boot, then the tale thrills with the threefold interest of victory over hindrances barring the path of the Jew, the immigrant, and the woman.

Out of these conditions arose the considerable number of autobiographies of Jews in the languages of many countries published since the middle of the nineteenth century. They explain why in America they have been written chiefly by the immigrant Jew, and why those written by Jewish women have aroused the keenest interest and discussion.

These memoirs by Mrs. Kohut strike a new note. They are all but unique in the American-Jewish autobiographical literature. They reckon with the milieu of the American secular life from an angle different from that occupied by the others written by Jewesses. The setting antedates that of the industrial nineties of the last and of the first decade of the present century. Not only have we the first American-Jewish autobiography by a woman past her thirtieth year, with achievement and experience to lean upon, but we have mellow influences to deal with instead of the harsh, callous grind of a mechanized life. Mrs.

Kohut's American roots reach down through the 1880s and 1870s to the generation that followed the Civil War. The patriarchal mode of living had not yet been completely disrupted. The South in which she spent her early American years was not so stricken but that the chivalrous traditions of a more prosperous past softened the asperities of impoverished and frugal households. And her California period palpitated with pioneering memories. The Richmond and the San Francisco of Mrs. Kohut's formative period bear as little resemblance to the Boston and the New York of the East European little Jewish girl, as Hungary and Russia are like America.

There is a still deeper-going difference between Mrs. Kohut's "Portion" and the narratives with which other American Jewesses have enriched both the American and the Jewish literature. Her memoirs do not carry us away from the Jewish milieu. Instead of the pathetic, inner estrangement between the generations on which the others dwell with painful insistence, or their equally pathetic straining after reconciliation between the elders and their children, Mrs. Kohut gives us a picture of the effective linking of the generations. While she lets us see her throwing herself with characteristic energy and zeal into the realization of American secular ideals, she remains at home on the Jewish scene. We are granted glimpses of a struggle with underlying principles instead of the usual rebellion against the burden of custom and ceremonial, which does not necessarily involve an inner alienation.

From the Jewish point of view it is of equal significance that she is impelled to set down her young woman's reaction to the conflicts between Rabbinical spokesmen that culminated in the Pittsburgh conference. Her own inner Jewish development and the inner development of the American Jewish community were of a piece. In general *My Portion* makes a contribution to the material at hand bearing on that notable period in American-Jewish history when the communal forces were crystallizing and their organization became the conscious aim, not of individual leaders only, but of the people at large. Indeed, as the reader travels along on the easy-flowing currents of the narrative, he finds himself wishing that Mrs. Kohut had put less restraint upon herself. He feels that she is keeping more in reserve than she allowed her memory to release. It is especially valuable to have her observations on the beginnings of the organization of Jewish women's endeavors, a movement which at this very time is flowering into a consolidation of Jewish women's forces of rich promise. The reader can but cherish and express the hope that the stores of personal experience still locked away, whose existence is betrayed by chance expressions, will be drawn upon more liberally for another narrative, even though it may have to be a narrative of less intimacy.

One would yield intimacy reluctantly, for whatever may be the historical value of these memoirs, the reader is chiefly grateful for the intimacy vouchsafed him with a warmhearted woman in her manifold experiences, placid and poignant, as daughter, sister, wife, and mother—an intimacy that admits him with frank hospitality to a close view of the shifts and delights of a rabbincal household, of the adjustments to the stepdaughterly and stepmotherly relation, of which *My Portion* is the epic, of Kohut the scholar in his sentimental moods, of all the varied interests, trials, and conquests over self and circumstance that have gone to make up a life of practical and spiritual striving.

The reader goes back once more to Glückel von Hameln. The interval between her and the diarist of to-day, measured in years, is two centuries. The two hundred years are annihilated when measured in terms of interests, of devotion to family, friends, and the public good, of wise activity and surrender of self. The feminine is eternal—the barriers of time fall at its touch.

HENRIETTA SZOLD

New York, March, 1925

My Portion

Chapter i

HUNGARY

AS I commence these reminiscences, the rain beats down in the courtyard of the New York apartment house in which I live. Somehow I have the illusion that this same rain is descending upon every inch of the world's surface.

The weather expert in the Whitehall Building may inform me that only a few miles away, across the Hudson, there are areas where the rain is not falling. I prefer my illusion. In my fancy the downpour touches every spot with which my life has been associated. It wrecks umbrellas and tempers in San Francisco; it drives people to shelter in Baltimore; it sweetens the streets of Richmond, Virginia; it drizzles gently in quaint little Hungarian villages of more than half a century ago—not war-torn, dismembered Hungary of the Versailles pact.

For this, you see, is a peculiar rain. It is not of this time and tradition. Its Richmond is one of white-blossomed magnolias and smarting rebel wounds. Its San Francisco is laid in the up-and-coming, free-handed seventies. Its Baltimore is the aristocrat of the last century. Its Hungary is that of the fevered days of Kossuth and alternate hope and despair.

An actual rain in Eighty-sixth street, New York, perhaps, but a phantom elsewhere. And phantom cities. And phantom people.

But it pours, and the eye sees sunshine. Faded flowers bloom again. Memory assumes a contemporary fury. A consideration of the past becomes my occupation of the present.

I believe I have a story to tell, activities to chronicle, my own as well as others'. In life there is love, and there is work. I have partaken greatly of both. In work I have had tasks, often against odds, that brought me into personal relationships with individuals whose lives are woven into the legends of America and of Europe. In telling my own story I may add to the record of theirs. I also chronicle the emergence of the American Jewess in the communal life of the country. This, I believe, is uncharted territory.

The Bettelheims are a Hungarian family. Originally the name was Bethlen; and how the family came by that name makes a story of medieval romance. In the town of Freystadt lived a Jewish merchant whose modesty gained him the esteem of his fellow-townsmen. As for his wife, she was so beautiful, so charming that her loveliness became a legend in the neighborhood. Count Bethlen saw her and was smitten. He tried to win her favor, and failing in his efforts attempted to use force. One day when she came to the market, in the sight of a hundred spectators, he seized and lifted her on his horse and, despite her cries of entreaty, was about to gallop off with her when her husband appeared. The two men fought. The husband came off victorious, and was ever after called the Bethlen-Jude. Years later when the Jews of Hungary were directed to take family names instead of the Hebrew form of nomenclature and they named themselves for mountains or orchards or occupations or the like, the Bethlen-Jude's family chose the name of Bettelheim.

Several generations later, one branch of the family espoused Christianity, while the other remained ever loyal to the ancient creed.

In the Jewish branch of the Bettelheims the sons have for centuries shown a predilection for the study of medicine or the rabbinate. It became a tradition for the oldest son to be either a rabbi or a physician. Sometimes, as in the case of my father, the oldest son would embrace both callings. Usually, if the boy became a physician, he was also well versed in the Torah and the Talmud; and the other way about if he became a rabbi. The Bettelheim tree accounts for seven generations of such professions.

Family tradition shone with most lustre upon one ancestor surnamed Leopold, who was a physician to princes and at the same time a Talmudist of no mean attainments. He was of the sort of physician about whom legends clustered in medieval times — the Jewish doctor who attended monarchs and, it was whispered, practiced magic. The "magic," of course, was nothing more than a thorough knowledge of the profession, reinforced by the sort of profound good sense which is a heritage of Talmudic learning.

When Leopold was physician to the Court Chancellor of Hungary, he was called into consultation about the mental illness of the Crown Prince. The heir to the throne had an obsession that there was a worm inside his thumb, an obsession only heightened and brought to the verge of madness by the insistence of numerous other physicians that it *was* only an obsession.

Leopold, when summoned, ostensibly agreed with the Crown Prince, and offered to remove the worm. The Prince was blindfolded, the thumb lanced, and the Prince then allowed to look. There was a little worm, but not from his thumb. The Talmudist doctor had taken it from an apple core. The Prince was cured.

For this and other distinguished services to the royal family and the nobility, the Jewish physician received a gold medal from Emperor Francis I, and was privileged to prefix a *von* to his family name—a privilege of which he did not avail himself. The medal is still a treasured heir-

Hungary

loom in the family and has acquired a tradition of its own; it automatically becomes the possession of the oldest male member who is a physician.

Another testimonial to Leopold Bettelheim's medical skill is in the form of a monument in the public square in the little town of Freystadt, Hungary, where it was erected in appreciation of his having saved the life of a woman whose body had been pierced by a carriage shaft in a runaway accident.

Distinction was not limited to the men of the family. My father's grandmother, Eva, was noted for her intellectual attainments and wide culture in a time when higher education for women was generally frowned upon. The last days of the eighteenth century—especially in Hungary, and particularly in Jewish communities in Hungary—were certainly not favorable to women who vied with the men for intellectual distinction. But Eva Bettelheim, who aided her husband in both his Hebraic studies and the management of his vineyard, was a learned Talmudist. More than that, under the encouragement of the famous reformer and evangelical pastor Hodze, she became a fine student of classical and modern literature. Up to the end of her long life, her active mind remained unimpaired.

My father, Albert Siegfried Bettelheim, the oldest son of his parents, was born the year the gold medal from the Austrian Emperor became part of the family tradition. Father was never the recipient of any sort of medal, but I fully believe that, granting the difference in circumstances, he was just as capable and deserving of one, if not so fortunate as his distinguished granduncle.

He was both a rabbi and physician, but it was not until he had brought his wife and six children to America that he commenced the study of medicine. His early training was for the rabbinate. He was a Presburg Seminary entrant at eleven, and continued his studies at Leipnik, Moravia, and Prague, his instruction at the latter place being guided by the great Talmudist, Solomon Judah Loeb Rapoport. One of his colleagues was Benjamin Szold, who was to become his lifelong friend.

A few years later he met the woman who was to be his wife, a widow with one little son. She seemed to him to have the same traits and endowments as his grandmother, whose memory he cherished. But the Jewish villagers of Komorn, where she lived, looked upon this woman with distrust, even ostracized her. She was too well educated, too enlightened. As a mere girl she had won their disapproval by being the first Jewess to become a school teacher in Hungary.

A little Jewish community in the '50s was hemmed in by regulations, by official decrees, forced in upon itself until its narrow horizon served for all the conceivable frontiers of life. That which had begun by being a restriction remained as a habit of mind. Poor, tortured, persecuted children! When sunlight came, they blinked. When freedom came, they had to learn the stride of freemen. When someone appeared who knew other cultures and thought them good, the cry was "Apostate." The great world outside was an ogre, and any one of their own people who moved in that great world was looked upon with suspicion.

The prejudice was definite enough when the object was a man. But a woman! It was against all tradition for a woman to be anything but subservient. And in the Jewish towns and villages of Hungary tradition sat unquestioned upon the throne, mighty, dictatorial. So we can imagine what was thought of this woman who chose the class-room rather than the kitchen for her sphere.

My father saw her trudging through the streets of Komorn, leading her little boy to school. He had been told about her, and his sympathy had been awakened before he had seen her. He understood. The walls of fanaticism did not enclose his spirit. He loved his own people, but not blindly; he knew other people as well. He had travelled, mastered languages, absorbed the cultures of civilizations other than his own. After obtaining his doctor's degree from the University of Prague, he had acted as Bohemian correspondent for London newspapers, and served as private tutor for Count Forgács, governor of Bohemia, later Hungarian Court Chancellor. At Temesvár he directed Jewish schools, at Czernowitz he was official translator of Oriental languages, and at Komorn he became superintendent of schools—the first Jew to gain such a distinction. And in Komorn he recognized in the widow a kindred spirit, loved her upon acquaintance, and asked her to marry him.

The people of Komorn and my father's parents disapproved. All sorts of pressure, family and communal, was brought to bear upon the young rabbi. They felt he was damaging his career by throwing himself away upon a widow—a widow with a child, a widow without a dowry. To this day the dowry exists as an institution in Hungary, a fact all over the Continent. Fancy, therefore, a brilliant young man who might marry a rich merchant's daughter chosing a life of poverty and struggle instead.

Though my father loved and respected his parents, their entreaties could not swerve him. The marriage was consummated; the couple settled down to life in Komorn. Still there was hostility all about them. They moved from Komorn to Kaschau, then to Freystadt. Five children were born in the last two places. Kaschau was my birthplace.

At Freystadt we were neighbors of Etelka Gerster, the famous opera singer. She became friendly with my mother and took such an interest in her children that she offered to give one of them, Minnie, singing lessons, believing that the little girl's voice was of promising calibre. An

Hungary

additional bond of interest between Etelka Gerster and our family was that we were cousins of Caroline Gumpertz-Tellheim, the beloved Viennese prima donna.

Hungary was torn by political and religious strife. The history of the Jews in Hungary since the ninth century had been one of persecution, expulsion, confiscation, burnings at the stake, with here and there an interlude of semi-leniency and "toleration tax." There had been kindly monarchs, too—such as Joseph II—whose brief periods of sovereignty afforded time to repair the ravages of the Colomans, Ladislauses, Corvinuses, and later the Hapsburg Leopold.

Then in the first half of the last century came Louis Kossuth, the great Hungarian patriot, the noble tribune of independence, who fought for the emancipation of subjugated races and extended a friendly hand to the Hungarian Jews. Bright was that sun of freedom under Kossuth. It was soon eclipsed, however. Victorious Hapsburg troops again swept through Hungary, making Jewish communities pay dearly for their support of Kossuth.

For two decades restrictions continued in force, until in December, 1867, a bill in favor of the emancipation of the Jews was passed by the Hungarian parliament. Following the emancipation, representatives of Jewish communities met at Budapest to consider the regulating of Jewish affairs.

Father, then at Kaschau, disagreed with the conclusions at some of these meetings, and was bold enough to say so in print. Whatever the particular points of contention, it required very little to bring down anathema upon his head. There was a storm of abuse, the fanatics in his own congregation held that his progressive principles were prejudicial to Judaism, and one of his former colleagues at Komorn went so far as to threaten excommunication proceedings.

The secretary of the Budapest Congress was a renowned young Hungarian rabbi and friend of Kossuth, named Alexander Kohut, sometimes called, because of his eloquence, the Jewish Kossuth. He and my father were to meet again under very different circumstances.

The fruits of the Budapest Congress were dissension and bitterness. But Father saw nothing of this. Saddened because of the various misunderstandings concerning his marriage and his religious views, he sailed for the United States, hoping to make a home for us there and enjoy respite from fanaticism.

He had been preceded in America by his classmate, Benjamin Szold, who became the spiritual head of a congregation in Baltimore. Dr. Szold came especially to New York to serve as the entire committee of welcome. He took his old friend back to Baltimore with him, and my father stayed under his hospitable roof for several days, until he received a call to Philadelphia, to minister to

Hungary

the congregation of the Crown Street Synagogue. A few months later my mother and her six children followed. The crossing in the sailing vessel, Austria, took us thirty days.

The two years in Philadelphia had little significance for the child of five to seven that I then was. But to my father, alive to the atmosphere of the New World, breathing the air of tolerance and freedom, glorying in the absence of fanaticism, they were years of joy. What if the salary was small and the parents had a hard time making both ends meet? There was the larger compensation of a new and stimulating environment, new friends, and a new language to master.

His first purchase in the United States was a copy of a daily newspaper. His second was a German-English dictionary. He read the first, word for word, with the aid of the second. Soon he was more American than the Americans. English, he insisted, must become the language of the household, though my older brothers and sisters found it easier to use their native tongue. Father, however, amiable though he was about most things, was unswerving in this. In Hungary he would have resented being forced to speak in English; but in the United States he considered English the only proper speech, and refused to be satisfied until he mastered it.

During the period of the Philadelphia rabbinate he became associated with Isaac Leeser, notable for his English translation of the Old

Testament and founder of Maimonides College in Philadelphia, the first Jewish seminary in the United States. My father became Dr. Leeser's colleague and taught classes in the seminary.

In 1869 he accepted an invitation from a congregation in Richmond, Virginia, to serve as its rabbi.

The Congregation Beth Ahabah (House of Love) had been formed in Richmond in 1841 and, after years of struggle, had enough congregants to provide funds for the building of a house of worship on Eleventh near Marshal street. It survived numerous disrupting influences and the hardships of the war.

"In 1867"—I quote from Ezekiel's and Lichtenstein's *History of the Jews of Richmond*—"the first steps in the direction of reform were taken, as evidenced by the following resolutions:

Resolved, that in the opinion of this congregation the time has come when a reform should take place; therefore, be it
Resolved, that a lecturer shall be engaged.
Resolved, 2d, that this Synagog shall be extended.
Resolved, 3d, that the Synagog shall be divided into family pews.
Resolved, 4th, that there shall be a choir in the Synagog.
Resolved, 5th, that the congregation has no objection to a melodeon being used in the Synagog, provided it is not at the expense of the congregation.

"A committee successfully carried out the resolutions, the lecturer engaged being the Rev. J.

Wechsler, who assumed charge of the congregation in August 1867.

"In January, 1869, the Rev. Mr. Wechsler sent in his resignation as rabbi, and Dr. A. S. Bettelheim was chosen as his successor, under whose leadership the congregation flourished. Minor changes were made in the ritual, and in 1873 it was resolved that the prayers should no longer be sung, but read by the minister."

In the *Richmond Dispatch* of September 6, 1869, appeared the following item:

> JEWISH CONFIRMATION.—The interesting ceremony of confirmation according to Jewish usage was performed at the synagogue on Eleventh Street, on Saturday morning. The subject of Confirmation was Marx Iseman, son of the postmaster at Spottsylvania Court-House, and Rev. Dr. Bettelheim officiated in a most impressive manner.

And in the same newspaper two weeks later:

> THE HEBREW FESTIVAL.—The recent solemn festival of the Israelites was observed strictly by those residing in this city. At the synagogues on Eleventh, Broad and May Streets, regular services were held, and largely attended. At the Eleventh Street synagogue the congregations were so large that sometimes no more seats could be obtained. Rev. Dr. Bettelheim, minister of this congregation, who has recently come in our midst, is a man of marked ability and eloquence, and has already attained great popularity with all classes of our citizens.

Chapter ii

RICHMOND

RICHMOND holds the most poignant memories for all of us, though we were there only seven years. Perhaps we were at the age of greatest impressibility. However that may be, we have always been enraptured by our memories of this city standing like Rome on its seven hills, with its streets lined with fragrant magnolias, and its people—impoverished though they were by the Civil War—still trying to keep up a tradition of courtesy in the grand manner.

It is the place my sisters and myself never tire of visiting. With each visit the flood of memory becomes enriched tenfold. And yet, while we were there, we had hardly begun our lives. It became our city of the spirit, enveloped in romance, Arcadia-like, bedecked in all the colors of youth and all the poignance of great sorrows which came to us before our sensibilities were dulled.

We arrived in Richmond four years after the termination of the war. The people had not recuperated. The war was still the chief fireside and table topic, bitterness toward the North was

Richmond

expressed in almost every breath. As the seat of the Confederacy, Richmond was full of memories of martial activities, of great personalities directing the government and the war machine, of wartime rationing and want and destitution.

In this fairest city of the South, so beautiful with its hilly vistas and its streets upon streets lined with magnolias and honeysuckle and walnut-trees, there was the after-war spectacle of extreme poverty and extreme wealth. The wealth was represented in those who had been successful blockade runners, eluding Union ships and Union soldiers and bringing food and ammunition and other supplies to the beleaguered South.

My father was welcomed by his new congregation, and commenced his rabbinate under favorable conditions. Many of the Jews of Richmond were people of fine aristocratic culture, and spiritually they had been uplifted by the sacrifice of the war period. Their interest in religion was vital. At Beth Ahabah my father found especially cordial and helpful the president, Moses Millhiser, and Rev. Dr. M. J. Michelbacher, who had been with the congregation as reader since 1848. I remember Dr. Michelbacher as a dear old man, a fringe of hair around his face, and wearing a very high choker collar, the sort I associate always with pictures of Thackeray. Far from Dr. Michelbacher and my father being rivals, they were great friends. Their duties did not conflict. One read the prayers, the other delivered the sermon. The children of the two families grew up together.

Soon after my father left Philadelphia to take up his new duties, two young members of the Richmond congregation left the Southern city to pursue their careers in Philadelphia. These were Samuel and Joseph Fels, the latter afterwards famous internationally as the wealthy supporter of Henry George's single-tax theories.

Once installed at Richmond, my father, with characteristic directness, enrolled as a student at the Virginia Medical College. There was great astonishment among neighbors when the father of six children was seen going off to school with his children every morning carrying text-books under his arm.

He had two reasons: he wanted to master English thoroughly, and felt that in the competition of the class-room, by being obliged to keep up with students to whom the language was as natural as breathing, he would accelerate his progress. The second reason was the family tradition. He was already a rabbi, he would be a physician as well, and embody the entire tradition in his own person. He would thus be the genuine healer, ministering to both the soul and the body.

What a marvellous man he was in his capacities for life! In addition to attending to the duties of his congregation and studying medicine, he found time to establish a weekly, write articles for daily newspapers, and make countless friendships. And

Richmond

his family—the time came when, in addition to everything else, he had to be both father and mother to us.

His friendships! He reached out everywhere, drawing to himself the best people of the community. There was that in him which made men respect and act in all sincerity with him.

Not by class or religion were his friendships made. They transcended all formal lines. He aided many Christian clergymen in the study of Hebrew. During the Richmond chapter he began a lifelong friendship with the man who was to become the most distinguished Catholic prelate in the United States. The late Cardinal Gibbons was at that time bishop of Richmond. He had come to Richmond in 1873 from Baltimore, and established himself in the little white wooden church across the street from our home at Marshall and First Streets. My father called upon him soon after his arrival, and from this call their friendship dated; a very real and sincere friendship.

As a child I used to watch the bishop go back and forth between our house and the little wooden church. In those days I always watched priests with fascination. Why, I wondered, did they wear such strange garments?

The rabbi and the bishop went into long discussions of various Hebrew texts, and spoke in friendly fashion of the problems of their churches. There was hardly an event of Jewish interest during my father's rabbinate in which Bishop Gibbons did not participate or display an interest. The lines of religion were not so tightly drawn then as they are today. Richmond was like a great big family town, unmarred by such enmities as have been introduced in later years through the activities of the A. P. A. and its uglier successor, the Ku Klux Klan. Later, when we moved to San Francisco, my father corresponded regularly with the Catholic dignitary, who returned to Baltimore, where he served subsequently as archbishop and Cardinal. They had often discussed the Passover blood libels, those monstrous accusations born of bigotry and ignorance, which have been a blot upon the history of civilization. Regularly, at the yearly recurrence of the Passover feast, my father sent the Cardinal a package of Passover cakes, accompanied by a note assuring him that no Christian blood had gone into their making. It was a stereotyped note, always worded the same way; and so was the Cardinal's regular acknowledgment, stating that the cakes had tasted very good. They enjoyed the yearly exchange of compliments, and joked about it considerably in later years when they came together again in Baltimore.

Cardinal Gibbons distinguished himself throughout his career as a prince of the Catholic church. In his writings and his life he proved himself a man of moderation and wisdom. I like to think that his friendship for our co-religionists, evidenced upon many occasions, was influenced by his association of seventeen years with my father.

Our Richmond home at Marshall and First Streets we regarded as a wonderful place. At the farthest corner of Marshall Street was the fine old home of John Marshall, Chief Justice of the U. S. Supreme Court, during the early years of the republic. Not far away is the Hollywood Cemetery, burial place of several American Presidents. It is to-day regarded as one of the most picturesque cemeteries, not only because of the quaint epitaphs on the gravestones, but because of the river which runs through the centre, banked by great weeping willows and the magnolia-trees without which no description of Richmond is complete. From this stream the water-power of the city's electric plants is developed. On each side are buried thousands of Confederate soldiers.

> By brooks too broad for leaping
> The lightfoot lads are laid.

Memorial Day in Richmond saw practically the entire population bringing wreaths. The womenfolk, especially, made great preparations for observance of this day. In the victorious North I have never seen such interest in Memorial Day. Had there been ten times as many graves, there would still have been enough roses and magnolias to decorate them all.

On Marshall Street, too, was the Negro congregation presided over by John Jasper, of "The Sun Do Move" fame. He was an evangelist who worked his congregation up to a pitch of religious frenzy. The expression "The Sun Do Move" was ever on his lips. Father discussed the solar system with the Negro pastor several times, but no amount of scientific explanation would convince him that the sun did not move. He was in love with his slogan, and with the reputation it gave him as a Richmond character.

Another character well known to the residents of the city was Grandma Sycle, familiar to all children, with her huge pockets that reached from the waist to the hem of her skirt—a curious fashion, or rather, not a fashion at all, but a war measure. In those pockets Grandma Sycle carried edibles for the soldiers, mostly fresh eggs and apples, and she was said never to have broken an egg, even when both pockets were full of them.

The school we attended was around the corner from our home. The teachers were daughters of once wealthy Southerners impoverished during the war. Though appointed because of their high social standing rather than for scholarship, they were efficient because of their deep interest in their pupils, with whom they established personal relationships. They seemed determined that the children, even if poor, should not be ignorant.

One little incident connected with our school life there and characteristic of my father and one of my older sisters clings to my mind. The pupils were expected to bring a few pennies once a month for ice for drinking water. My sister happened to tell that one of the girls was too poor to give even a single cent, but she had shared her ration of iced water with her. My father was delighted and gave his generous daughter a generous reward.

Another incident of those days, of a rather opposite nature, also remains with me vividly. On the many occasions that I have returned to Richmond, I have always gone to visit the tree about which the event centres, an immense walnut-tree half-way between our home and the synagogue which my brother Felix and I used to climb to shake down the burrs. Once we chose a Sabbath morning, when we were supposed to be on our way straight to synagogue. Up in the tree we did not see our father coming, and a great rain of burrs showered down directly in front of him. He just missed the deluge; he did not miss the naughty children; and the children did not miss their punishment. I will not describe it, but it was adequate.

When the city instituted the system of public schools in 1871 the congregation offered the class-rooms of its building rent free. The city accepted, and the first public school in Richmond was located in the synagogue of which my father was rabbi. Prior to this, there had been a private school, described two years earlier as follows:

RICHMOND GERMAN, HEBREW AND ENGLISH INSTITUTE.—This first-class school, under the auspices of the "Congregation Beth Ahabah," will commence its session on Wednesday, the 8th instant. It will be under the control of the Rev. Dr. A. S. Bettelheim, late of Philadelphia, at present rabbi of the above congregation, assisted by a competent corps of teachers—among them Mr. William Y. Sheppard, Jr., a native of this city, and Miss Lucy King, so long and favorably known as principal of a first-class female school. The terms of the school will be very moderate, it being the object of the founders of the institution only to realize a sufficient amount to defray expenses. As only a limited number of scholars will be taken, we advise all to make early application.

The very first year in Richmond, my mother became ill and grew steadily worse. The cares of the household devolved upon my oldest sister, Esther.

One duty of the Jewish housewife my dear mother clung to with tenacity. Every Friday afternoon Esther led all the children to her bedside to assure her that we were prepared for the Sabbath eve services. Mother would look at us tenderly, then, with great effort, lean over the bedside, light the Sabbath candles, and pray over them. The candles were then brought into the dining-room, and back to her bedside when the evening meal was over.

Young as we were, we realized that all was not well and were filled with awe as we looked upon her thin arms and the shadows upon her face as she prayed over the candles.

The day after they buried her, on a Friday

evening, we sat on the stairs quarreling as children in a family will. Our father appeared and in a low and grief-stricken voice told us to come to his library. He was white-faced and grave. We followed him in silent wonder. With himself in the centre he formed us into a circle, placing us according to age, and told us to hold hands.

"Little motherless ones," he said, struggling with his emotion, "I place each of you in charge of the other. You must each guard the one who is younger than you, and you must always try to keep the circle unbroken. As long as you do that, I will have no fear for you." He tried to say more, but his emotion overcame him, and he hurried from the room.

The scene made a deep and abiding impression upon the older children; and by iteration and reiteration, as the younger ones grew up, the wish of my father became the keynote of our family relations. Family unity has been a sacred and hallowed responsibility with us, due to the poignant manner in which it was first made significant.

It seemed as if the whole of Richmond gathered at the house for the funeral. All our friends were there, as well as the members of the congregation. From the Christian churches of various denominations came many clergymen. The Catholic priest and the Protestant minister joined in expressing sympathy with the rabbi in his bereavement.

They buried our mother in the Jewish cemetery at the top of Shockoe Hill. On Sunday afternoons we visited our mother's grave, and decorated it each time in a new and what seemed to us a more beautiful way. We played games there, too. For this we were chided by friends, to whom it seemed to be bad form to be happy amid such surroundings. The cemetery, though, seemed to be the one bright spot in our lives, and we had the feeling that here our mother was near us. And when we returned home towards sundown we were happy, even though many considered us wrongdoers.

The cemetery overlooked a deep ravine. At the bottom was a large iron foundry, from which, at night, the flames threw a weird illumination upon the graves. The sight fascinated me, and often in the night Felix, Minnie, and I would steal out of the house and stand on the summit of Shockoe Hill, staring enchanted.

The cemetery is between two alms-houses, one for whites, the other for Negroes. The Richmond people used to speak of the irony of the location; the paupers had no outlook except upon graves.

Part of the cemetery was railed off as a resting-place for Confederate Jewish dead. This plot, known as the Soldiers' Section, was enclosed with a railing of so impressive an appearance that it has been described in numerous magazine articles and books. Furled flags and stacked muskets are represented on the posts, surmounted by the Confederate forage cap. The design of the railing between the posts, repeated at innumerable intervals, consisted of crossed swords and sabres, wreathed with laurel. There has been no end of comment concerning its emblematic appropriateness, imaginative conception, and artistic details. One could almost vision soldiers there, guarding the graves of their comrades. The designer was Major William B. Myers, son of the remarkable Gustavus A. Myers, who was the most prominent Jew in Richmond. The father died during our first year in Richmond, and was mourned by all classes of the community. Playwright, legislator, newspaper owner, leader in many public welfare movements, and enjoying the largest legal practice in the history of the Richmond bar, he was beloved by all. He was a friend of Jefferson Davis, president of the Confederacy, and an intimate of Judah P. Benjamin, the South's Secretary of State.

One of the Richmond Jewish youths who served with distinction in the Confederate Army afterwards won world renown as a sculptor. Sir Moses Ezekiel, creator of the great Arlington Memorial and of many highly praised sculpture groups to be seen in European and American galleries, left the United States to become one of the most distinguished residents of Rome.

Management of our household, in addition to his lonesomeness and all other cares, was too much for my father. In course of time he married again.

But his marriage produced no schism in the family. We always remained a devoted group, each of us ready to shield, and make sacrifices for, the other. The children of three different mothers got along amazingly well. We loved our stepbrother Paul most of all, and many a time I have forgotten which was my stepsister.

My new mother was a very real contribution to our family life. She completed the process of Americanization for us. A native Virginian, she was the daughter of a wealthy tobacco planter who had become impoverished by the war and the emancipation which set his two hundred slaves free. In marrying my father, she went from poverty to poverty, but always retained her alert mind, her caustic wit, and her aristocratic manner and temperament. She was permeated with the tragedy of the war, through which she had lived, and was exceedingly bitter in her hatred of the North. The difference between her family's station before the conflict and the adversity in which it was now enmeshed was one to which she could never become accustomed. We all loved to listen to our stepmother's colorful stories of ante-bellum Virginia and the splendors of her girlhood. Her account would be punctuated by caustic allusions to the Northerners. Her comments derogatory to the Yankees were continued even after we had shifted our home to the

West. Father always endeavored to steer conversation clear of the war. While he was conscious of the suffering it caused and the bitterness it engendered, it was more remote to him than to those who had participated in it, and he saw no good in keeping the controversy alive by discussion.

We children spent two summers at Waller's Tavern, the home of our new grandfather. He was not only the manager of his plantations and former slaves, but also the postmaster and general storekeeper at Spottsylvania Court-House, and the only Jew within a radius of many miles.

Waller's Tavern was at the crossroads between Spottsylvania Court-House and the road to Fredericksburg. Near by flowed the Rappahannock. The Court-House was a mile up the river. Many of the most memorable battles of the Civil War were fought in this vicinity, notably the engagements of Chancellorsville, Spottsylvania Court-House and the Wilderness. It was there that the Union Commanders, Hooker and Sedgwick, faced Lee and Stonewall Jackson. Both armies crossed and recrossed the river many times. One of the reasons why the local residents were so particularly embittered was because hundreds of Confederate cavalrymen were drowned with their horses in the Rappahannock when Union troops cut below Fredericksburg and forced their opponents to cross. Spring torrents had flooded the Rappahannock above its banks, bringing disaster to attempts to ford the stream. It was just as bad for Union cavalrymen, but the neighborhood saw only its own losses.

During the war Waller's Tavern was occupied in turn by both Union and Confederate soldiers.

Vivid in my memory is the Tavern, with the darkened musty parlor used only on special occasions and the rest of the time occupied by nothing but the horsehair furniture and wax flowers. To be debarred from that parlor was no hardship to us. We much preferred playing "store" in my grandfather's shop, exchanging eggs for calico, just as he did—trading in the literal sense of the word. Very little money changed hands. The standard of currency was eggs.

Waller's Tavern seemed palatial to us, and the lavishness of the table could not fail but impress. For all his dwindled fortunes, my grandfather, a true Southerner, did not make readjustment and exercise rigid economy.

We stayed in what was called the "new house," a one-room dwelling detached from the Tavern. We thought it wonderful, but always entered with trepidation because of the many hornets' nests around the windows.

I shall tell of my literary studies, of my lectures on English poets and novelists, of my familiarity with the works of Goethe and Heine, and my love for certain American books; so I think it only fair to say that at Waller's Tavern, at the age of eight or nine, my literary nutrition consisted of the Police Gazette. I found copies

Richmond

of it in the attic, as also Godey's Lady's Book, in which I proceeded to read the sensational accounts of the trial of Henry Ward Beecher upon the charges of his former friend, Tilton. I must admit with shame that I read and re-read the Police Gazette reports of the trial. The following year, after Dr. Beecher was acquitted, I experienced a guilty feeling about my literary taste, and confessed to my father. He told me that I must not read at random but should ask to be directed to suitable literature.

My acquaintance with the Police Gazette was never resumed. I have been told it is not quite so lurid as in earlier days. Godey's Lady's Book has become so rare that copies command extravagant prices at book sales. Collectors of intellectual literature are willing to pay even more for them than for first editions of McGuffey's Fourth Reader.

The most important man in the vicinity of Waller's Tavern was Colonel Day. Everyone spoke of the Day mansion, and used the expression "as rich as the Days." We, too, decided he must be fabulously rich, for when we visited the Day home we saw baskets and baskets of eggs on the back porch. Colonel Day himself was a dashing individual. As we walked almost daily up the road that led to his house, we often saw the Colonel surveying the world from the back of his best saddle horse—features sharply aquiline, long, sweeping mustachios, goatee, wide slouch hat.

Reading Colonel Carter of Cartersville years later, I felt F. Hopkinson Smith must have known Colonel Day. Perhaps there were thousands of Colonel Days or Colonel Carters, mint juleps, "By God, suh's," stogies, exaggerations and all. This Colonel Day had wonderful horses and dogs. His home, they said, was a gathering place for sportsmen; and all the little niceties and grandiloquences were observed. He exploited his slaves when he had them, but he knew how to make them love him. I saw on many occasions free Negroes, who had been his slaves before the emancipation, prostrate themselves upon the ground when the Colonel came dashing along upon his horse.

There were many things said of the Colonel, some doubtless in malice, others out of esthetic appreciation. He was said to have a way with women. It was mentioned in a quieter key that he had a large uncatalogued progeny conservatively estimated at one hundred. Conjecture, this. What was fact was that his two spinster sisters kept house for him; and suddenly, at the age of seventy, he decided to marry.

We children remembered vividly those paths overgrown with big red patches of sumach and the most wonderful flowers. It was only a few minutes' walk to the Day mansion, but we usually consumed hours, what with picking flowers, eating berries, and fascinatedly watching the army of tumble-bugs industriously rolling balls of manure. How thrilled I was five decades later when the two beetles came rolling in their "pile" on the stage in the insect comedy *The World We Live In*.

Forty-five years after our stay there, my sisters and myself decided to visit Waller's Tavern and see what Time had wrought. The building was still standing. On the porch sat a toothless old Negro almost blind. Upon being asked if anyone living in the neighborhood knew of the Iseman family, he replied: "Yes, I done remember Marse Isaac Iseman." Then, a moment later: "You know, Miss Winnie, she died last year." He was referring to our little stepmother, though I do not recall how he learned of her death, as we had been living in the North many years. The old man was over ninety.

We entered the house and saw the parlor, just as musty as in our time, and with two of the old pieces of furniture remaining. But the spacious store of our childhood had shrunk woefully. Oh, what a small building! Fearfully disconcerting. Had we imagined with our children's eyes the place bigger than it was; or did old buildings shrivel up like old people when the sap and purpose of life were gone and the Last Call is imminent?

Over those once beloved roads we walked, hoping for the magic key of association with our youth. It was unfamiliar ground, its character had changed through constant neglect. Human activity seemed spent, and Nature had set decay to to work to change the aspect of Man's early toil. The old trees were gnarled, scrub apples their only fruit. Though the last generations of the Days still lived on the land, distinction had fled, and life was hard and uninviting. With children attending school only three months of the year, illiteracy, too, was becoming a factor.

Life is movement, and constructive energy travels in cycles. Residents of Waller's Tavern had moved elsewhere and commenced anew. And on the way from Fredericksburg we saw the prospering little homes of immigrants who had left European equivalents of Waller's Tavern and by the transfer found in themselves the stirring of creative energy.

Chapter iii

WESTWARD WE GO

MY FATHER entered into a second marriage because he was unable to occupy himself with the cares of the household. Within a few years, however, the new wife, too, became an invalid, and it had to be with the assistance of the "little mother" of the household, my sister Esther, that we were carefully reared until we reached the age of self-help.

Arduous burdens, a small salary, congregational cares, home duties—these might have been enough to weigh heavily and affect my father's fine nature. Yet they didn't. He remained as active and alert as ever. He had amazing energy, a marvellous capacity for diversified interests, a great love of humanity as a whole and individually. And in the family he combined the father's authoritativeness with a mother's tenderness. In the outer world, however, he had no will to advance his personal and material interests.

A scholar, possessing all the potentialities for literary achievement, he left behind brilliant fragments, interesting monographs on medicine, three-quarters of a revised American Bible, but no great, complete, unified memorial of scholarship. He had the scholar's mind without the scholar's aloofness. The door to his study room never remained shut for long. There were too many conflicting demands upon his time and energy. Many of them he could have ignored, but he loved human contacts and was happiest when he was helping others.

Such talents as he possessed he could not commercialize. If he wrote for newspapers, as he frequently did, it was because of his interest in the subject, not for the possible remuneration.

It was the same with medicine. His object in studying it was not an eventual prosperous practice, but to make himself like one of the healers of old. He wanted to minister to the poor. His rabbinical charge, he felt, was something more than presiding over ritual and preparing a sermon. But his congregation did not see eye to eye with him on this. They objected to his medical and literary activities, and to his plans for the education of children. Putting through an educational programme was always a struggle.

A rabbi's life was no sinecure. To his family it was an especial trial. You never knew when you would be called upon to uproot yourself and move elsewhere. The rabbinate was not so stable as it is to-day. The trouble lay mostly with the "business" side of congregations, which were largely interested in drawing worshippers from other congregations. In this they expected help from the rabbis. My father could not bring himself to it; it was extremely distasteful to him. Once his flock even met in secret to consider asking for his resignation because of a heinous offense of which he had been guilty. The father of one of his wealthy congregants had belonged to another synagogue. When he died, his son left our congregation to join his father's, and my father approved. A serious matter. Congregants were few, each one counted.

A pall usually settled upon our family in the summer when the renting of congregational pews began and it was learned that some family had decided to worship elsewhere. But my father loved human beings whether they worshipped at his synagogue or not, and he cherished theories which were not conducive to prosperity. Here may be the appropriate place to tell that a well-known artist in Richmond painted my father as Jesus.

Today many rabbis are elected to their posts for life. But in the 1870's the rabbis might have been classified as floating population. It was difficult to keep track of the wanderings of some of them. Only a few Jewish communities were large enough to build temples and offer stable, inviting opportunities for capable men.

The state of California was at its period of greatest romantic appeal, and the glamour of the Golden Gate, radiating over the entire country, touched my father, too. The West allured with the many tales of the land flowing with milk and honey. To be a pioneer, or almost a pioneer, was a pleasing thought. He saw as his own duty in such a world not the hewing of roads and the building of houses for people to dwell in, but the building of a spiritual house in which souls might dwell. His thoughts of California were induced by a venturesome spirit rather than by a restless nature. So, when simultaneous calls came from congregations in Hartford and San Francisco, he chose the latter. After seven years in the dear old city of Richmond, he pulled up stakes and with high hopes turned his face west. He left several months in advance of the rest of the family to prepare our new home for us.

In the early autumn of 1875 we bade farewell to Richmond. At that time it took ten days to cross the continent—ten days in a railroad train! Our party almost filled one coach, as we were accompanied by a bridal couple and two boys whose parent had entrusted them to our custody. There was no dining-car service, so we were obliged to carry along our own food. The members of the congregation had donated huge hampers filled with foodstuffs, and at each stop we hurried off the train for hot coffee. How we ever escaped spells of indigestion is a mystery.

The journey was enlivened by our anticipations and fears. In the imaginations of the boys and girls of that decade the place of the "movies" was taken by harrowing tales of Indian warfare. The tribes were resentful over the many new railway lines that cut through their stamping-grounds. It was a year before the Custer massacre. As our train left the East, my brothers, at each curve of the track, expected to see Indians. As a matter of fact their apprehensions came true; on two different occasions Indians discharged arrows at the train—probably a gesture of resentment rather than a desire to do definite harm. Yet the act had its effect upon us. I was convinced that the Indians were as ferocious as I had been told. Later my notions were upset in a distressing manner. I was left without my perfected design of the universe when we found other Indians peacefully selling beads at Cheyenne and other stations.

The little house on Larkin Street, which had been furnished us by the congregation, seemed palatial. In delight and wonder we began our acquaintance with the city which only a few years before had been El Dorado.

San Francisco afforded the most vivid contrasts. Half of the city was still sand-hills; other districts gave all the appearance of a well-built city, conscious of itself and anxious to appear to good advantage. It was the most cosmopolitan city of America. One could see members of almost every nationality on the streets. It presented the curious anomaly of crudity and sophistication, of rough free-handedness and an attempt at culture. Chinatown was squalid and Barbary Coast sinister, but San Franciscans preferred that attention be given their art-galleries and libraries, their flourishing social and literary clubs, and their public school system, which ranked third in the United States.

Though only the shadow of the fever af '49 remained, placer mining was still attracting prospectors from the East. The day of the orange-grove was beginning. At California seaports the wooden sidewheeler had given way to iron and steel propeller vessels, the "Colima" being the first of the new steamships to be launched by the Pacific Mail Company.

A young city, San Francisco already had tradition. The '49 rush and the period of the Vigilantes had gone into history, and native historians were vying with one another to chronicle those times. The men who had participated in the gold epic and who had emerged triumphant were ensconced in magnificent mansions upon the heights, and engaged in the business of acquiring dignity and tradition. Those who were not as fortunate adjusted themselves to the commercial life of the new city or went under. Such stories as were told!

Amazement and delight were my first reactions to California. Almost everyone carried flowers. Almost every house, however rude and humble, was decorated with flowers. The glory of Richmond was in her magnificent trees and her rose-bushes; in San Francisco one's eye met floral beauty in every form, without the wonder of it ever palling. The variety of California flowers, the profusion of them, the people's appreciation of them, colored life gloriously. The calla-lilies grew in great hedges around the homes of the humblest, and covered the ugliness of wooden fences. Geraniums and heliotrope, vine-trained, were used to hide the rough walls of huts.

Our home boasted no garden in front. It seemed almost a symbol of poverty that no flowers grew about the place. But there were always plenty inside the house, and always enough to take in bouquets to our teachers.

The oversupply of weather in San Francisco made an immediate impression upon our young souls. In the course of one day we experienced not four seasons but six. It was some little time before we grew accustomed to the various motifs; before we took it for granted that winter would express itself through cold winds in the afternoon; that this would be followed by the heavy fogs which rolled in from the bay and made traffic difficult; that these would roll away and give us clear starry nights which made us glad we were alive.

My father immediately became an active member of the community. He wrote for *The San Francisco Call, The Chronicle, The Argonaut;* became identified with prison reform and the anti-vice crusade; organized a society for the study of Hebrew by Christian clergymen. Several times he was asked whether he would serve on the board of education, but he felt his hands were already too full. He was still interested in medicine, and had just taken up service in a new congregation. But above all he was occupied with his Hebrew studies. He was working upon a revised English version of the Bible, and was in regular correspondence with the great scholars of Europe and America.

Our home was the gathering place of an interesting group. All sorts of people came to us, among them many striking personalities. Michael Reese, who had been a resident of Richmond and later left $200,000 for the construction of the Michael Reese Hospital in Chicago, was a frequent visitor, though he had the reputation in his lifetime of being a recluse. Miss Apponyi, a California member of the famous Hungarian family of that name, exchanged memories of Hungary with us. John Swett, superintendent of public schools and one of the original Forty-Niners, became a dear family friend. Toby E. Rosenthal, afterward one of the most distinguished Californian painters, received at our home encouragement which was instrumental in making possible his first trip to the studios of Europe. Adolph Sutro was frequently in the Larkin Street house. Sutro was a name to conjure with in San Francisco in the seventies and eighties. Who did not know of Sutro, of Sutro's Gardens and Sutro's Baths, of "Mount Parnassus" and the famous Cliff House? He collected a magnificent library of rare books and precious manuscripts and decided to donate the library to the city and provide a building to house it. His visits to our home were for the purpose of consulting my father about various Oriental and Semitic manuscripts.

An intimate clerical friend was the Rev. Dr. Guard, whose son, William J. Guard, is the best-loved official of the Metropolitan Opera House.

Shortly after our arrival in San Francisco, Isaac M. Wise came to the city in behalf of the Union of American Hebrew Congregations. He became not only our guest but my father's inseparable companion during his stay, and we children got to adore him. This great man, who so thoroughly imposed his personality upon American Judaism, was a delightful talker and full of fun. Dignity and command were his, but not austerity. He encouraged us to be intimate with him. And our ease in his presence was in delightful contrast with the solemn reverence we had been taught to show our elders. In Richmond he had fascinated us by relating many of the incidents of the war that he had witnessed, and of his various pilgrimages to the great Lincoln. His time and efforts had been spent in behalf of Jewish soldiers, though he had emerged from the civil conflict more American, perhaps, than many of the descendants of the Mayflower passengers. Only a man of his striking personality could have so large a following as his. As almost mere babies, I recall, we responded to the magnetism of the man.

We liked to hear him talk, and to look at his wide expanse of brow, and his head which was so huge for his body, and the eternal spectacles perched upon his forehead, and worn under his hat. (Even on photographs the spectacles appear upon his forehead.) His sermons, as we heard them in later years, were given in an almost conversational style and at once drew his hearers into intimate relationship with him.

The remarkable thing about the relation between Isaac M. Wise and my father was that they remained close friends in spite of the differences in their attitude towards Reform and Orthodox Judaism. The conflict between Reform and Orthodoxy concerned itself chiefly with changes in the Jewish liturgy and the ceremonials of the synagogue and the home. The reformer shortened the public service by the excision of the prayers dealing with the ancient sacrificial service and its restoration in a rebuilt Temple on Zion. He favored the use of the vernacular almost to the exclusion of the Hebrew language in public and private worship. He introduced the organ into the synagogue, and abolished the women's gallery and the separation of the sexes during the hours of worship. In general, he showed little mercy to customs and festive and mournful commemoration days based upon the Rabbinical tradition in contradistinction to the Biblical law. But, repudiating the Rabbinical institutions, he came to lay less and less stress on the dietary laws,

Westward We Go

even though they were rooted in the Mosaic law. The most radical went so far as to advocate the transfer of the seventh-day Sabbath to Sunday. Thus Reform cut deep into the heart of Jewish life, and not rarely caused enmity between brothers and friends. It is therefore noteworthy that the friendship persisted between my father and Dr. Wise, who was one of the extreme Reformers.

During our first days in California we children entertained the fallacy that we were rich. This was because of the currency. The huge silver dollars in which our father's salary was paid, gave to our youthful imagination an impression of correspondingly huge purchasing power. Rattling in his pockets, they sounded like the mint or a declaration of dividends. The mere sight of the mountainous pile lying in the upper bureau drawer was enough to make us enthusiastic about the rabbinate, given such gingerly recognition in Richmond and such liberal recognition in San Francisco.

When the rabbi's dollars left the house, however; when they careered along the wooden sidewalks with the market-basket, or fell under the assaults of the clothier or bookseller, they seemed to go into some shark's mouth, like minnows, without putting up any sort of a fight, without even first having made an impression.

We were poor. The five girls and two boys in our home insisted upon growing bigger and bigger every day. Dresses passed from larger to smaller children, in the transition acquiring patches and other marks of service. But we were not to be so conscious of our second-hand clothing and patched shoes as of our second-hand school books. Childish pride told us we should be able to purchase new text-books like other pupils, not used volumes which advertised our poverty. My over-sensitiveness in this regard caused me intense suffering as a young girl.

Almost everybody except ourselves seemed to be enjoying wealth. What was wealth? The power to buy new school books and ride to school instead of trudging blocks and blocks and climbing hills in the rain; the power to own a dress which was not handed down from sister to sister; the power to take lessons and go on picnics. The life-story of any dress in our family could be divided into five chapters, each chapter headed with one of the five sisters' names. How often we wanted the story suppressed, or discontinued after the first chapter; but circumstances insisted upon spinning out the tale to its conclusion.

Although our poverty and shabbiness made no difference socially, since we were the Rabbi's children, yet my sisters and I were really unhappy. We blamed the congregation. We felt it stood between us and contentment. There was such a marked contrast between what, to our mind, was a rare human being and the compensation that was granted him. The root of the trouble was that San Francisco had too many congregations, and none of them thrived. This also had a bad spiritual effect. On account of the unhealthy rivalry among the congregations, they were more concerned with membership drives than with higher values. My father, so much a man of warm human contacts, was sickened by the petty competition, and chose lay associates rather than the company of local rabbis.

My brother and I often spoke of the situation, and in our adolescent way we expressed very decided views not only as to Jews and Judaism but as to rabbis as well. We did not see the other side of the picture. These groups were having their own struggles. Only inherent love for the faith kept the congregations alive. We did not realize, either, the common tendency of the heterogeneous groups—among Jews as well as among Christians—to consort with others of their own temperament and identity of origin. Just as in Richmond there were the Polish, Sephardic (Spanish-Jewish) and Ashkenazic (German-Jewish) congregations among the Jews, so in San Francisco, to an even larger extent, people divided themselves into groups according to their European backgrounds.

My younger brother, Felix, was enrolled in the University of California. As between medicine and the rabbinate, he had chosen the former for his future career. His father's wish was that the boy prepare himself to be his successor, but Felix did not feel the spiritual call strongly. His impatience with the congregations was transmuted into antagonism against the ministerial service. To his mind his father was not appreciated. The boy did not realize that this was of less moment to his parent than to himself.

As my brother and I walked the hills of San Francisco to our respective schools, we formulated the platforms for our future, and one of the important planks was: No poverty. We were thus running counter to one of the family's pet obsessions. Its members waxed sentimental about poverty, about its ennobling virtues, about the wicked rich and the good poor. It was my habit to argue, in rebuttal, that the rich were not always wicked, nor the poor always good.

For every person who comes unscathed through poverty, there are a dozen others upon whom it places its mark; whose spirit it crushes, and whose outlook it warps, leaving them twisted, unhappy, embittered creatures. And so for myself I decided against poverty. I hate it because it is the most deadly enemy of all—the parent of vice, ignorance, mendacity, crime.

And yet I have been poor a large part of my life.

Chapter iv

GROWING PAINS

FATHER'S study was in the basement of the house. On pine shelving from ceiling to floor fitted against each wall stood his books in Hebrew, German, English, Sanskrit, Persian, Arabic, books on all subjects, medical as well, arranged in orderly rows like captains, corporals and privates, standing at attention. The long table was piled with newspapers and open volumes, evidence of the owner's constant association with literary and scientific research. My father did not require the quiet of the cloister for his studies; he could concentrate upon his work with a half a dozen of us about, and he allowed us to use his room for our study room also. He encouraged us, in fact, to browse there all we liked, and never labelled certain books as forbidden fruit. Excellent modern psychology that for one of his generation.

We soon learned how to use the reference books, but always supplemented our information by interrogating Father, who was glad to help us. His methods of teaching, however, were often at variance with current school methods. Nevertheless our teachers had great respect for us because there was someone at home who took such pains to prepare us for our school work.

And the preparation of our school lessons was a joy, certainly by contrast with our practising on the piano. For despite our limited means, we were given musical instruction, the belief having then prevailed—does it exist to-day?—that no young women could be considered cultivated and refined unless she could play the piano. Tedium, thy name is piano practice. I, for one, absorbed this sort of refinement under protest.

The library became the meeting-place of the family. For me it served the purpose of the drawing-room in a mansion. It was the one place to which I brought my friends, as it was the one place where poverty was not in evidence. One night judge from it that we were both rich and wise. I enjoyed the snobbery of it.

It was not long after we were established in San Francisco that I began to broaden my wordly knowledge by eagerly reading the periodicals, dailies, weeklies, monthlies, religious and secular. But my reading had all to be saved up for Saturday and Sunday, the week-days being taken up with school studies. So how to get the most out of Saturdays and Sundays became a problem. I had to appear at the temple Saturday mornings; then I was pressed into service to teach religious school, at which pupils were only one or two years younger than myself. And there was so much

Growing Pains 51

that I wanted to read, so many things about town that I wanted to see. For instance, there was the sensation of the moment, Dennis Kearney, the sand-lot agitator, the demagogic spouter who sought prominence by, among other things, pronouncing himself the friend of the workingman and inveighing in thunderous tones against the Chinese. Every speech of his closed with "The Chinese must go," a slogan suggested to him by a newspaper acquaintance. My brother and I, having heard of the crowds that packed his tent to cheer his war-cry and curious to know what it was all about, went to his meetings on Saturday mornings before attending the Sabbath services. My father, strongly against such appeals as Kearney's to the baser passions of the mob, would have rebuked us sternly had he learned of our presence at the sand-lot meetings.

It was my dissatisfaction with the congregation and my duties toward it that brought me, by not altogether pleasant ways, more leisure to read and improve my knowledge. During divine service on the Sabbath, instead of following the prayers, I read the Bible, and at Sunday-school instead of teaching catechism, I used what I liked from the Bible as the subject-matter for instruction. The catechism was the only teaching manual allowed Sunday-school teachers in those days, and one morning, when the chairman of the school-board visited the classroom he was surprised to hear me telling the story of Ruth.

"Why are you not teaching the catechism?" he demanded.

Hotly, disrespectfully, I replied: "I teach what I please."

When he left the room I realized that my father might be an innocent sufferer from my outburst, and went home heavy-hearted. Surely enough, he was called to account for neglect of the Sabbath-school, and I was dismissed. Of course, I was fearfully sorry and repentent that my father should have been involved. Yet the bit of leisure was a great joy, and one of the direct results was an enlarged knowledge of American history, in some respects also revised knowledge; for San Francisco's version of the Civil War differed widely from Richmond's. Between the two influences, the Union finally dominated in my receptive mind, despite my mother's continued bitterness. The San Francisco schools and a performance of *Uncle Tom's Cabin* made me an ardent believer in the righteousness of the Union cause.

Imagine, therefore, my excitement when I was selected as the representative of my class to shake hands with General Grant, the Union's military genius, at a reception to him in Mechanic Pavilion, in which the school children participated—the supreme honor. And I hurried home breathless with the news, forgetting for the moment my mother's intense antagonism.

"Go upstairs and wash that hand," the little

rebel mother remarked grimly. But—in 1920 my mother cast her vote for the Republican party, the party of Lincoln and Grant.

And that human document, *Uncle Tom's Cabin,* which so moved the hearts of millions— what has become of it? As a stage presentation it has been relegated to burlesque. We smile over it. However, old stage methods may seem grotesque and ridiculous, yet the drama of the human heart is ever poignant, and new hates always spring up afresh to try the human soul. People may laugh at Uncle Tom, Topsy, Simon Legree and Little Eva; let them laugh, if they will, at the Ku Klux Klan.

Fridays nights at home were devoted to singing and story-telling. Forgotten were the little cares of the week. My father would have us be like a guild of singers, with himself as choirmaster. There was nothing he liked better than to direct the chorus and hear the hearty outpouring of our voices. He himself contributed a baritone of considerable volume, and among the girls it was the rich contralto of my sister Minnie that sounded best. After the singing my father's talents as a story-teller were called into play. He never failed to delight us, and we could listen to the same thing over and over again. Several of the tales he told us were published in *The Argonaut* and received high commendation for their interesting subject matter and charming style. Our favorite was the one he called *The Man With The Marble Heart.*

It must not be imagined that we were a closed family circle on Friday evenings and Saturdays. On the contrary. My father, with his big, expansive nature, believed in sociability, and wanted us to broaden our outlook through having many friends. The family's meagre purse did not prevent our entertaining a great many people. My father would have been unhappy had he not been able to act as host. Every year, at the Passover festival, he had us invite our friends and teachers to our home for the first two evenings of celebration, the Seder services, they are called. They were memorable evenings. Usually there were about forty or fifty guests, a great many of whom were Christians.

Once I asked my father why he invited Christians.

"To let people see that we have no secrets," was his reply. "You can be made to believe fantastic things about people when you do not know them. But when you know, you cannot be misled. So many lies are manufactured about us—especially in regard to Passover—and they gain credence among the unthinking and the ignorant. But those who know us will see that these are lies. Throw open the doors and let people view us as we are. In this way we dissolve antipathies and make friendships, and when efforts are made to defame us, we will have friends who will champion the truth."

This was his policy throughout his life. The individual friendships contributed to the general good of his people. But his valuable work along these lines did not always receive appreciation from people of his own religion. Men who preached clannishness and exclusiveness were not wanting in Israel, and they were ever quick in their blind demagoguery to attack him for his friendships with Catholics and Protestants.

Not only was he attacked for the good work he was doing; narrowness went even further. In some mid-Western city—Cleveland, I believe—there was a converted clergyman named Bettelheim. By some strange method of reasoning, certain members of the congregation arrived at the conclusion that my father should be held responsible for the religious beliefs of all the world's inhabitants bearing his name. A meeting was called, and the indignant rabbi subjected some of his narrow-minded congregants to a severe flaying which they did not forget for some time, and which cleared the air permanently.

My father and his "Christian" relative became good friends through correspondence and exchange of photographs, and very recently I learned that it has been suggested to establish a memorial to him as the first Protestant missionary to China.

Across the street from the temple was a bakery.

The baker's son, Julius Kahn, was my brother Felix's intimate friend, and visited us frequently. He became one of my father's favorites. Julius Kahn's ambition was to be an actor, and he undertook earnest study for the stage. My father did not discourage him, but said he believed he would advance to a wider stage and do more important work than behind the footlights. In following Julius Kahn's life, we experienced the satisfaction of seeing this prediction come true. The young man was on the stage for several years, then entered political life and was elected to Congress as a representative of California. He became one of the ablest legislators in Washington. His constituency returned him to office again and again, and he was given legislative responsibilities of increased importance. As senior Republican member of the military affairs committee of the House during the Great War, he drafted the bill calling the men of the country to the national service.

Another young San Franciscan of Jewish parentage, destined to become one of the great actors on the American stage and a still greater producer, was beginning a stage career at that time, with the Baldwin Theatre Stock Company. My father had known David Belasco's father when David and his brother, who also went in for acting, were mere lads, though the family lived at a distance from us, on Howard Street, in a part of San Francisco which, like New York's East Side, has produced some of the best human material. I recall the furore when the Baldwin players were arrested for giving a performance of Salmi Morse's *Passion Play*, which Belasco had staged and acted in. Another player in the cast was James O'Neill, famous for his portrayal of the Count of Monte Cristo. Mr. O'Neill died about ten years ago. Had he lived a few years longer he could have enjoyed the sudden ascendancy of his son Eugene to a foremost place among American dramatists.

My first year at high school was a period of torment to me. The junior class of high school was located in a building only two blocks away from Chinatown. The proximity to this quarter, then branded as dangerous for young girls, aroused in me a peculiar spirit. I hated everything that made it necessary for me to go near that morbid part of the city. I hated the school, the teachers, the educational system, the hilly streets I had to trudge, while well-to-do friends rode, the rain, the German professor's accent. Poor Professor Sanger! Had he seen some of the notes I indited about him. Poor professor indeed! He was recognized in after years, at the University of California, as one of the greatest educators on the west coast.

School, once a haven, became a prison to me. Ordered one day in the history class to prepare a composition upon any subject I pleased, I chose, in a spirit of sheer recklessness, to write a sarcastic essay on the unsuitableness of the school building, the unfitness of the teachers, and the incompetence of the board of education. The essay shocked the teachers and was transmitted to the principal of the high school, who happened to be my father's friend, John Swett.

"The style is good," he commented, amusedly. "Which shows that the teaching isn't so bad." Then he disciplined me by expelling me from the history classes for the rest of the term. Father taught me history at home.

It was a critical time for me. I was not naturally rebellious, but everything in the educational scheme seemed especially designed to irritate me. And there was no understanding teacher or friend at school who brought out the best in me, no one to command my respect or reverence.

The second year at high school, however, saw a momentous change. In a different building, located in a different section, I breathed more freely. The teachers seemed better, the subjects more interesting. Fled was the morbidity induced by the nearness of Chinatown with its frowsy white women sitting at the windows of Chinese homes.

What had the greatest effect upon me was my friendship with the class teacher, Caroline Lora Hunt. No teacher before had given me sympathetic understanding. Hers was the influence I needed.

There were two things that had brought us together; on her part interest in Jews and Jewish history, on my part the autograph craze. Miss Hunt directed our after-school reading and formed her pupils into a literary club to which we contributed weekly for the purchase of books. At the end of the term the books were distributed, and as a special mark of personal interest in me, she sent a copy of the *House of the Seven Gables* to Hawthorne, whose cousin she was, with the request that he inscribe it for me. Needless to say I prize the copy among my most precious possessions

Miss Hunt was small and stout, with lovely blue eyes. In the days of Montague curls, kept flat on the forehead with bandoline, she wore her mass of hair brushed straight back. Altogether her appearance and manner were simple, and her gentleness, especially, contrasted markedly with the ways of one of my teachers at the other school. She had, too, a sparkling sense of humor and a fund of anecdote about her Puritan ancestors that was both interesting and instructive.

Without any apparent effort, she called out the best that was in me. Her inspiration caused rapid strides in my development. My knowledge and capacities increased, my sympathies broadened and deepened. Altogether, I was transformed from the sarcastic fault-finder of the year before.

When I think of my adolescent adoration of Miss Hunt, I am not inclined to laugh at myself. She was truly a rare human being, worthy of anyone's admiration. Of course, lover-like manifestations are always funny. I used to walk up and down the street in hope of catching a glimpse of her, and saved up pennies to buy her flowers, and often, after sitting up all night making poultices for my sick mother and going to school discouraged and depressed, it needed but a nod of recognition from her to buoy me up and the merry twinkle in her eye to carry me happily through the day.

She was the cousin of another famous writer, Helen Hunt Jackson, author of *Ramona*, and took me along on her visits to her. Like Bret Harte, Helen Hunt Jackson was a venerated name in the West, because of her pæans to the Rockies and her popular novels about California. At that time she was an invalid and had chosen to spend her last days among the hills and wild flowers near the Golden Gate. It was in a spirit of awe and reverence that I accompanied Miss Hunt to the novelist's home, and with joy that I received a copy of *Ramona* with her autograph.

Miss Hunt's interest in me and my family led to her meeting my father and taking up the study of Jewish History under his guidance. She also came to one of our Seder services.

Another fine influence in those days was my friendship with my classmate, Emma Wolf, later a brilliant authoress noted particularly for her story, *Other Things Being Equal*. She and I used to roam the sand hills together on botany excursions.

Growing Pains

Botany was in our curriculum. Is music in the curriculum for larks? How could one live in California and not become a botanist? Saturday afternoons and Sundays we went over the hills of Saucelito and San Rafael, yellow poppies around us, carpets of maiden-hair ferns under our feet. The sand-hills of California! Who can forget them? Mountain high, uninhabited for blocks and blocks, with little oases of wild flowers breaking up their bare, desolate vistas.

One of eight daughters, Emma Wolf, was handicapped from birth by a useless arm, but there was no defect in her mentality. Her memory was the most remarkable I have ever encountered. She could quote with equal facility the texts of long poems or the fatality statistics of each of the world's great battles.

On our walks we hunted for new specimens of flowers, which we took home and mounted. We vied with each other in trying to get together the largest and best collections. I also sketched flowers, which I had learned to do not from an urge to artistic creativeness, but from mere love of beauty. Those walks, indeed, did a great deal to stimulate our sense of beauty.

But what meant most of all to me, perhaps, in those impressionable days of adolescence, was the exchange of innermost thoughts with my classmate. I had begun to doubt the worthwhileness of all the sacrifices it seemed to me that my father and his family were making for Judaism. What was the use of it all, I questioned. Why make a stand for separate Jewish ideals? Why not choose the easier way and be like all the rest? The struggle was too hard, too bitter.

Emma Wolf was undergoing much the same inner conflict. It meant real suffering to both of us. The spiritual growing pains of adolescence are hard to bear. They cannot be laughed out of existence.

Chapter v

SPIRITUAL TRIALS

YES, religion oppressed me. I had been both rebellious and irreligious for a year, and felt keenly the material limitations of a rabbi's life and a rabbi's home. That a man with such breadth and abilities as my father should be so burdened and harassed was beyond my concepts of justice. It seemed to me he was always being called upon to do gross things, and it was not until later in life that I realized how fine were his acts and how much he was elevated in his thoughts above material things.

We usually gauge our misfortune by the other person's good fortune. When we are unhappy, someone else's happiness serves to make our own state more acute. One of my schoolmates who accompanied me on sand-hill expeditions was Clario Hobart, a Christian. I became a frequent visitor to her home, and was profoundly stirred by the spirit there, and devotion to an ideal. Never had I seen such beautiful home life. Her people were devout Christians, and happiness and gentleness fairly radiated from them. I looked beyond my own people and my own religion, and I saw that others were good. Especially was I dazzled when I thought of my father's unappreciative congregation. And as I meditated the thorny path which the Jew travelled, it seemed to me that if the Jew could assimilate with the Christian, many of his irksome trials would be eliminated, with no spiritual loss. Of course, I did not know at that time the word "assimilate" in its racial or religious usage, but that was my thought. In the latter years of my life, I have grown eloquent in my arguments against that which I so warmly advocated for myself in my San Francisco girlhood.

I wanted to discuss with someone—preferably a person outside the family circle—the questions which were troubling me. An opportunity came during a walk with Miss Hunt. The conversation touching casually upon religion, I mentioned my debates with myself, and courted her opinion. Miss Hunt was not only a devout Christian, but she had studied Jewish life, and she tried to prove to me that it was a glorious thing to be a Jew and suffer for an ideal.

Father did not know of my frequent visits to Clario Hobart's home. I was not afraid he would object, but felt intuitively that I was drifting from my bearings and was fascinated with the idea of picking my own course to safety. The day came, however, when I told him. Clario Hobart was to be married and I was to be her

Spiritual Trials

bridesmaid. He objected to my serving, and in the ensuing discussion we exchanged our views fully. "You know," he said, "that you'll never marry a Christian, and there is no real reason why you should seek the homes of Christian friends in preference to Jewish homes. I object to your attending the ceremony not because of your friend but because of yourself."

That was the end of that episode. He knew his children, and felt that decisiveness upon his part was the only way to check any action based upon immature speculation.

On graduating from high school, I entered normal school, and came under the supervision of the second woman who was to influence my youth. The principal, Mary Kincaid, was a schoolmate of Phoebe Hearst, to whose generosity the University of California owes its establishment. Mary Kincaid was a woman of unusual ability. Physically, her angular appearance and long nervous stride attracted attention; mentally, her knowledge, forcefulness, quick mind, and sympathies made her unforgettable. I soon enjoyed the privilege of her companionship. In school she maintained a distance between students and herself. This was policy rather than temperament. But after school, in long walks, she revealed herself to me in all her human sympathy. She was very inquisitive about the customs and ceremonies of the Jews, and was anxious to receive first-hand a description of their home life.

Frankly she asked me if I was proud of being a Jewess, and just as frankly I told her that I was emerging from a soul struggle, involving my religion. This struggle was my own secret. Since the day my father had expressed himself so emphatically, I had not spoken of my religious doubts to anyone. Nevertheless, I had carried on a continual debate with myself. My father, though he knew what was troubling me, refrained from probing into my soul.

From the moment I confessed my uncertainties to Mary Kincaid I was unconsciously influenced by her to return to the religion of my people and embrace it wholeheartedly. She showed me that they needed me, that there was work to be done in their behalf which was more important than the state of my soul; and that through doing this work devotedly and unquestioningly, I would acquire a finer soul than if I were merely preoccupied with the question of—my soul!

If in thirty-seven years of privileged service among my own people and others I have bettered my soul, I say: Let me not forget Mary Kincaid.

My first experience in social welfare work came when I was invited to serve on the Fruit and Flower Mission of San Francisco, an organization of young women to collect from the well-to-do and give aid to the sick and poor. Its membership was entirely Christian and the recipients of its aid entirely non-Jews. I was happy to be the bearer of bounties to the poor.

Spiritual Trials

It was my love for flowers that made the work of the Mission doubly precious to me. The most wonderful specimens were sent in by carloads daily. We would spend the entire day prior to making the rounds in fashioning the huge bouquets, striving for combinations that would bring out the colors most delightfully. The flowers lay in mountainous heaps at the mission headquarters; certain varieties required the space of an entire room each; and it was a pleasure to feel that one could be lavish with nature's gifts.

Serving the Mission, I made regular visits to an old Southern lady whose only child had wandered off with Confederate soldiers, never to be heard from again. This poor old soul, suffering from infirmities of age, living in direst poverty, took it upon herself to make a good Christian of me. Her belief in her faith, her spiritual happiness despite all that had befallen her, was almost unsettling in its power. I wondered why Jews could not find joy in their religion to the same degree as did Christians. Several incongruities forced themselves upon my attention; the Bible and the prayer books urged us to rejoice in the Lord; they spoke of the joy of life and the beauty of the world; but the Jew saw only sorrow. On the holy days in the temple he beat his breast, his voice quivered with the sadness of the memorial service. That anguish of soul which is so truly a part of the Jew in his history was in marked contrast with the poise and cheerfulness of the Christian.

As I grew older and came back, as it were, to the faith of my fathers, I realized only too well that Judaism was not the cause of this sorrow, but rather Christianity. Especially during my last visits to Europe after the war, and my experiences in Austria and Poland, has it been brought home to me with increased conviction that Jesus was an expression of the idea of Judaism. The Jewish people have been crucified millions of times.

I visited my elderly Christian friend one Sabbath morning before going to the synagogue, and found that she had died during the night. She lay in angelic peace. After notifying the authorities and making arrangements for her funeral, I hurried to the synagogue. As I read my prayers, I thought of my dear old friend, and the feeling came to me that she had gone to the same heaven that held my mother, and there could only be one God for us all.

The experience with the Fruit and Flower Mission was succeeded by kindergarten service. The kindergarten idea, originating in Switzerland, was introduced in the United States by Professor Felix Adler. In preparation for our work as teachers, one term at the normal school was given to practical field work among children. It was my good fortune to be assigned to the Perry Street kindergarten, conducted by Kate Douglas

Spiritual Trials

Wiggin, later famous as a novelist, and her stepsister, Nora Smith.

The Smith girls, or "Miss Kate" and "Miss Norah," as every one called them, had become imbued with the kindergarten idea soon after Professor Adler introduced it. They went to New York to study under his supervision; the instruction completed, they proceeded to Switzerland, and observed the movement at its source. Then, fully equipped, they returned to California and opened their kindergarten in Perry Street, in the heart of Barbary Coast, that strange polyglot section of San Francisco infamous in song and story as the resort of the seamen of the Pacific.

There was a marvelous relationship between the two stepsisters. Miss Kate was an ethereal, golden-haired creature, a spinner of dreams. Miss Norah, tall and angular, was a better executive. They chose to go into the vicious Barbary Coast section because their work was most needed there. The district was full of waifs, homeless and motherless, whose eyes saw squalor and vice every day of their young lives. The young women welcomed these waifs to the kindergarten. They came timidly and suspiciously at first. When they saw, however, that they were treated with kindness for the first time in their lives, their little hearts responded. At daybreak Chinese children left their homes and hurried to the kindergarten to be with these two beautiful women and their assistants, who washed and fed them, and sang wonderful songs and related marvelous stories. Sobbingly, they protested at being sent home at night.

Many years have passed since that first San Francisco kindergarten was founded, but the textbooks, songs and stories compiled by these two sisters are still the standard works all over the world. Miss Kate's entry into literature was by way of the stories she wrote for the entertainment of the children in the Perry Street institution. It was not long before her unusual talent was discovered and appreciated. The young woman's class grew larger, it included adults as well as children, and was numbered by the hundred thousand; it was nothing less than the great American reading public, which knew her as Kate Douglas Wiggin instead of Miss Kate.

In New York, years later, when her story *Rebecca of Sunnybrook Farm* was produced upon the stage, I went to see it three times. I can find much in my own life to parallel that of Rebecca's, who grew up with a mortgage and was always trying to work out of the difficulties that life had imposed upon her.

In addition to the studies at normal school and field work at the Perry Street kindergarten, I had two years at the University of California, specializing in English literature and history. At that time there were not many women students at the University, which had become co-educational only a few years before.

Spiritual Trials

When the trustees of the congregation learned that I was pursuing a higher education, they expressed considerable objection. It was almost as strange to them as my mother's learning had been to the little communities in Hungary. They spoke to my father of their disapproval, and warned him that it was dangerous and altogether too radical to allow one of the opposite sex to imbibe the higher knowledge.

My father's view was different. He wanted each of us to have a university training. I took courses all the time I was in San Francisco, only ceasing when prevented by an illness of several months' duration.

A third teacher whose personality acted as an influence upon me was Fidelia Jewett. Truly feminine, beautiful, with golden hair and charming voice, she proved to be a surprise. Aloof in the class-room, this apparently cold and statuesque beauty was a different being outside of it. She was not only full of love and kindly feeling towards people in general, but she was especially desirous of a better understanding between Jew and Gentile, and expressed herself upon this subject many times.

Slowly and unconsciously, through the influence of these three women, and with the careful guidance of my father, I became spiritually stronger than I had expected. Pride was felt in one's race, glory in one's religion, sublimity in its martyrdom. I became overproud as I thought of

Israel's mission. Yes, I was a true member of my family, extremely emotional. Our tear glands were usually responsive; we wept rather readily.

"The best history is biography." Unconsciously that was the method I used for the study of Jewish history. It had been disconcerting to find that Christians like Mary Kincaid and Caroline Hunt and Fidelia Jewett knew more about Jewish history than I did. It was time to catch up. As I learned of the careers of some of the great women of Israel—of the Mendelssohn daughters, of Sarah Copia Sullam, Deborah Ascarelli, high in the councils of the Italian Court, of Rebecca Gratz, most beloved and honored woman of her time, who served as the model for Rebecca in Scott's *Ivanhoe*, of Emma Lazarus, equally beloved a century later, of Grace Aguilar and a host of others—a new pride possessed me. More cause for worship, more examples of nobility, richer race consciousness. These Jewesses, they had saved Judaism and perpetuated it as well. What would they be like today? Comparison suggested itself with the women of the day who were fighting the battle for the emancipation of their sex.

The woman's rights movement in America was acquiring momentum and significance, ridicule notwithstanding. Cartoonists might caricature Mary Walker, and men laugh at her because she wore men's clothing when she appeared before Congress to plead women's rights. But the cause

Spiritual Trials

couldn't be laughed out of existence. Mary Walker, continuing to wear trousers and a high silk hat on a lecture tour throughout the United States, was the visual expression of women's discontent with unequal suffrage. Lucy Stone, Susan B. Anthony and Elizabeth Cady Stanton were promoting the cause of millions of their sisters in the face of widespread opposition. Julia Ward Howe and Harriet Beecher Stowe were names that meant much.

I associated the work of these women with the history of the women of my own people, and found much similarity in their ideals and aspirations. Deborah became to me not a prophetess but a great political emancipator. Mother Sarah stood for the single standard of wife and mother in the home. What I learned of the Jewesses of the past caused me to feel the burden of responsibility devolving upon the Jewesses of the present and future.

My ambitions to work for equal suffrage received further impetus through the agitation that was carried on by various persons to grant citizenship to the Chinese and Japanese of the West coast. I held that American women were entitled to recognition first.

Study of the history of the Jews led me to a realization of their position as a minority. I arrived at the view that we had a mission as a protesting minority, and a protesting minority must be ready to suffer. As for myself, no matter how wide my interests might become, and how intensely I felt everything that affected the United States, it appeared to me that my real mission in life should be as a worker in the front ranks of American Jewish womanhood.

There were no conflicting aims in my program as I mapped it out. It was possible to be fully devoted to both religion and country, which were not in any way opposed, but rather dependent upon each other.

We were now in the 1880s, and several members of the family could consider themselves quite grown up. My brother Felix had been graduated from medical school and received an appointment as ship's physician of the Colima, making the Pacific Mail run between San Francisco and Panama. He was the pride of the family, and loved by every one who knew him. Talented, conscientious, considerate, handsome, he was expected to win distinction in his profession. He did not disappoint his well-wishers. He became resident surgeon of the Panama Canal under De Lesseps and was instrumental in having the first general hospital built there.

Just before my brother left San Francisco, my oldest sister was married. Her husband evinced a lively interest in all the members of our family, and made it his business to provide us with theatrical entertainment, which was beyond our purse.

San Francisco attracted all the leading players. I saw Edwin Booth in *Hamlet*, Lawrence Barrett in *Hamlet* and *Francesca Da Rimini*, Tommaso Salvini in *Othello*, and attended the lectures of Henry Ward Beecher.

When Adelina Patti came to San Francisco, the people lost their heads. They waited day and night in line to purchase tickets. The most desirable seats commanded fabulous prices. I felt keenly the pangs of poverty when I heard of rich girl friends who had orchestra seats. But at four o'clock on the day of Patti's opening performance in *Il Trovatore*, my brother-in-law came to our house triumphantly waving a couple of tickets. They were for seats in a stage box; he had given a hundred dollars a piece for them. One of the tickets was for me, he said. My father was horrified by the extravagance, but I was tremendously excited and joyful. That evening poverty was only theoretical.

So great a crowd was expected and so heavy was the traffic of coupés and barouches, that we started for the opera at six o'clock, although the performance was scheduled for nine. The strain of the excitement had been too much for me. Patti was Patti and a stage box was conspicuous, but my head began to droop. My brother-in-law saw that I was napping, and woke me up. It was an expensive nap.

My brother's absence from home drew my

father and myself even closer together. Because I had become interested in Jewish history and perhaps because I had become more companionable, my father allowed me to spend many hours in his library with him. But now that I had delved into the past, studied its leading men and women, noted its events, I was to be made familiar with the present. Father asserted that Jewish history, significant Jewish history, was being made at that very moment, in America.

Jewish congregational life in the United States today is not the controversial thing it was in the 1880s and early 1890s. Though it still has its alignments, they are not nearly so sharply drawn nor so bitterly contested as they were three or four decades ago. It was the period of white heat in the battle between Orthodoxy and Reform. Rabbis thundered, personalities were bandied. We have seen a similar alignment during the last few years between the fundamentalists and modernists of the Protestant church.

It was with the controversy between Orthodoxy and Reform that I was now made familiar. The names of several of the main contestants were already known to me. Marcus Jastrow and Benjamin Szold I knew as my father's former colleagues in Europe. Isaac M. Wise, the storm centre of the conflict, the father of American Reform, had been known to us since early Richmond days. Constant mention of the names of

Spiritual Trials

Dr. Max Lilienthal and Dr. Bernhard Felsenthal of Chicago—my father's correspondents—made me almost feel I knew these men, too. The brilliant sermons of the young Chicago rabbi, Emil G. Hirsch, were discussed in Jewish circles throughout the country.

Isaac M. Wise's genius lay in his organizing powers rather than in scholarship. Two monuments to his creative and executive capacity are the Union of American Hebrew Congregations and the Hebrew Union College. The success of these institutions was an implicit challenge to Orthodoxy. The influx of Jewish immigrants in the early '80s had necessitated the establishment of many new congregations. Coincident with this, the Hebrew Union College was each year sending out as graduates a number of young rabbis schooled as advocates of extreme Reform. They were for overthrowing everything Orthodox and discarding all the traditional ritual. Led by such able lieutenants as Emil G. Hirsch, David Einhorn, and Kaufmann Kohler, the young Reform rabbis ridiculed and furiously attacked Mosaic Judaism. Outraged Orthodoxy seemed to lack the militancy necessary for coping with its foes. The Reformers appeared to be carrying the day, changing the entire age-old aspect of synagogue service, borrowing from other creeds, dispensing with things hallowed.

In this controversy my father, as I have already

said, was a conservative or perhaps he might have been called a progressive. Opposed in Hungary for not abiding by every last portion of ritual, he was himself opposed in America to such an absolute turn-over as the radical Reformer was trying to consummate. Though he knew that ritual could not forever remain static, he insisted that change must be gradual. In the traditional services were many beautiful ceremonies which constituted an unbroken chain between the modern Jew and the Israelites of the Old Testament. These had held the Jews together in their times of greatest adversity. They were the chief solace and source of strength when the Jews were surrounded by enemies. In dispensing with them, with no adequate and reverence-inspiring substitute, an irreparable loss might result. He was against it, and criticized the Reformers from his pulpit.

I followed the entire conflict in the organs of the contending factions.

One day I read that a great Hungarian scholar and preacher, Dr. Alexander Kohut, had after much persuasion accepted a call to America to preside over the destinies of one of New York's largest congregations. His coming was heralded with jubilation by *The American Hebrew*, which in leading editorials and other places in the paper proclaimed that at last Orthodoxy had its champion; that the radicals would find an opponent

Spiritual Trials 79

of a different mettle in this world-renowned scholar and magnetic preacher.

My father had not yet seen the announcement. When I brought it to him, he was charged with excitement.

"Wonderful news!" he cried. "A great man and a great scholar. Look, here is some of his work." He took several big volumes from a shelf, and explained to me that this work, which he called the *Aruch Completum*, had been hailed by scholars the world over as one of the most important and epoch-making contributions to Jewish literature. He then related to me how the scholar had been toiling over these volumes—parts of a gigantic Talmudic lexicon in Hebrew—for twenty years.

"A great man, a great preacher, a great scholar," my father went on enthusiastically. "A friend of Kossuth. In Hungary they loved him. He was recently appointed to the Hungarian parliament, and he is the Jewish light and pride. And something else"—laughingly—"he became the secretary of the Budapest congress which I criticized."

Thus my first knowledge of Alexander Kohut. We looked forward with interest to his arrival, and to the ensuing effect upon the religious schism.

In *A Memoir of Alexander Kohut* Barnett A. Elzas has described illuminatingly the conditions then prevailing.

80 My Portion

Kohut arrived in New York on May 3, 1885. The joy of his new congregation was unbounded. His arrival was everywhere acclaimed with the utmost enthusiasm. A new light had come to American Israel.

Judaism in America was in a parlous state. The scientific spirit of the day was manifest in all the affairs of life. The writings of Lyell, Buechner, Moleschott, Charles Darwin, Tyndall and Spencer, which had played havoc with the Church, was playing no less havoc with the synagogue. Indifference to all things Jewish prevailed everywhere. Ethical Culture, Christian Science, Spiritualism and the various occult movements were winning an ever-increasing number of adherents from within the ranks of Judaism. In some reform pulpits, the cherished traditions of Israel were openly flouted and a dangerous Universalism was being preached. The Abrahamic Covenant was denounced as a relic of barbarism, a Sunday Sabbath advocated, and the dietary laws declared to be only antiquated superstitions. The latest utterance of the last-printed scientific book was the religious pabulum of many Reform congregations.

A good vocabulary, combined with elocutionary graces and the ability to speak without a foreign accent, were the main assets of the younger Jewish Reform preachers. The older Reform preachers, of European birth and training, and European traditions of learning, were fast losing their influence.

Such were the conditions when Kohut arrived. The Orthodox pulpit had not produced a single man strong enough to call an effective halt and to stem the tide. True, there were able men in the conservative pulpit—Jastrow, Szold, Morais, Bettelheim, Mendes and others; but their influence was limited to their own congregations. With the advent of Kohut the tide began to turn; and to him is largely due the fact that the tide did turn. The action in recent years against the vagaries of the extreme Reform that characterized the early Eighties is in no small measure to be attributed to his published utterances and the controversies with the advocates of Reform to which they gave rise.

Spiritual Trials 81

The first public utterance of the new leader was awaited with eagerness by friend and foe. For they saw him not merely as the new leader of a congregation, but as the recognized spokesman of the Judaism of tradition. If his first words were intended only for the limited sphere of his congregation, they would nevertheless be given a wider significance. All Orthodoxy would look for a rallying cry; and Reform, expecting a challenge, would try to take the measure of the new opponent and find vulnerable points, if any.

The strange thing about the entire situation was that Alexander Kohut was not Orthodox. A leader of the Conservative division of Judaism, standing on a middle ground between Orthodoxy and Reform, he sought neither "the way of fire" nor "the way of snow." Perhaps the best designation of him would be as a conservative Reformer, "offering the old and the new in happily blended union." But Orthodox Judaism saw in him a champion of traditionalism, who would lift up his voice in denunciation of extreme radicalism in religion.

Without the Hungarian rabbi's knowledge, the stage had been set for a conflict. Polemics, I learned later, were abhorrent to him; nor did he relish the thought of having a battle thrust upon him. But bitter words had passed back and forth anent his coming, and his entrance was akin to that of the principal character in a drama.

So Alexander Kohut spoke; and his words,

intended primarily for his own congregation, were read by Orthodoxy for support and by Reform for challenge. "We cannot maintain Judaism without tradition," he stated. And Reform prepared to throw down the gauntlet to him.

Dr. Kohut's impassioned humanism and sense of justice are amply illustrated in the following extracts from his first discourse:

> A reform which seeks to progress without the Mosaic rabbinical tradition is a deformity—a skeleton without flesh and sinew, without spirit and heart. It is suicide; and suicide is not reform. We desire a Judaism full of life. We desire to worship the living God in forms full of life and beauty; Jewish, yet breathing the modern spirit. Only a Judaism true to itself and its past, yet receptive of the ideas of the present, accepting the good and beautiful from whatever source it may come, can command respect and recognition.
>
> But let us guard carefully against heresy-hunting. It is worthy of note that the first moral truth enunciated in the Ethics is this: "Be circumspect in judgment."
>
> We believe that we represent true Judaism. Let us not excommunicate the leaders and members of other congregations who maintain a different standard. While we may deplore the fact that each swings his censer of separate religious view, let us realize that everyone must strive after truth in his own manner. Let us learn tolerance from the rabbis of old, so often and so unjustly decried as intolerant, who said: "Israel is to be likened unto the pomegranate; even the seemingly insignificant among him is full of virtue and humanity, as the pomegranate is full of seed."
>
> How much that is good and humane is practised by the Reformers. Our false Orthodox (sincere and honest Orthodoxy is tolerant) who are so ready to use harsh words and who would deny the Jewish name to everyone who differs

Spiritual Trials

from them in opinion, should judge with greater leniency the Jewish heart that dispenses charity. Where the Jewish heart still beats, Judaism and Jewish piety are not extinct. Therefore, "Be circumspect in judgment."

Not his the words of a demagogue, but of one who treated his opponents with consideration, crediting them with sincerity of motive, but at that time indicating the rocks and shoals toward which they were heading.

His address had scarcely been uttered when Reform answered him. Its spokesman was Dr. Kaufmann Kohler of Temple Beth-El. The Kohut-Kohler controversy will some day loom as one of the most significant episodes in American Jewish history. It was felt by many that the challenge to Dr. Kohut, so soon after his arrival, placed him in the embarrassing position of a newcomer criticizing residents of the country which welcomed him. The Hungarian rabbi replied, but he fixed the plane for the discussion so high that personalities were banished, the conflict becoming one of principles. In the tense feeling that prevailed in both camps, it would not have been difficult to stir up passions and crown Fanaticism king. But Dr. Kohut's fair-mindedness was disarming; it banished invective and made it possible for two men of differing opinions to cross swords in a manner befitting their dignity and character.

In San Francisco we followed the Kohut-Kohler controversy in every phase, as Jewish families did everywhere throughout the country. If the controversy was free from invective, it was none the less spirited. That dangerous possibility in scholars' arguments, pedantry, was, happily, missing. It was an interesting dispute, and led to many fierce side-encounters between protagonists of both factions. Jewish newspapers such as *The American Hebrew* of New York and *The American Israelite* of Cincinnati, Dr. Wise's organ, featured little other news. They published attacks and counter-attacks in full. Practically all of the rabbis of the country devoted their sermons to the same subject and drew large attendances. Dr. Kohut's Temple was packed to the doors each time he spoke.

So ably did he state the case for traditional Judaism that the Reformers for the first time fell back to entrench themselves. For the first time they felt the necessity to meet the arguments of a strong opposition. So they called a convention to formulate a plan of campaign. This convention, known in American Jewish history as the Pittsburgh conference, is generally conceded to have been due mainly to the effectiveness of Dr. Kohut's espousal of the cause of traditional Judaism.

The Reformers at the conference went farther than ever before; they drew up resolutions by which they divorced themselves definitely from the Mosaic creed.

But the resolutions proved to be a boomerang.

Spiritual Trials

They displeased a number of leading Reformers, among them Dr. Gustav Gottheil, of Temple Emanu-El, New York. Many of their own adherents were shocked. As for the Orthodox, the effect upon them was not what their opponents had calculated. They were strengthened more than ever, and their unity expressed itself in a constructive manner, now that they had a leader.

Isaac M. Wise, the foremost Reformer, had been responsible for the calling of the Pittsburgh conference, and Isaac M. Wise was the head of the Hebrew Union College. Rabbis trained at this college could but reflect the views of its mentors. Therefore a new theological seminary, to represent the Orthodox, was necessary. Such a seminary had long been the dream of several ministers, but it had seemed an unattainable vision. The combination, however, of Orthodox unity, Reform audacity, the Pittsburgh conference, brought a new seminary within the range of possibility. In the light of the urgent need, financial help and organizing enthusiasm were forthcoming.

Alexander Kohut was the direct cause of the Pittsburgh conference, and the conference was the direct cause of the Jewish Theological Seminary in New York. Dr. Sabato Morais of Philadelphia and Dr. Kohut were its principal organizers. Oddly, both these men, reared in different environments, were in analagous relationships with heroes and statesmen of their native countries. Sabato Morais, Italian born, was the intimate friend of the great Italian patriot, Mazzini. Alexander Kohut was the friend of the great Hungarian patriot, Kossuth. Mazzini and Kossuth—names written large in the annals of liberty. And Morais and Kohut! in the annals of American Judaism they stand out.

Chapter vi

NEW YORK

THERE were other controversies besides religious ones. Railroad expansion was the order of the day, and the efforts and conflicting ambitions of the "empire builders" often resulted in rate wars.

Both the Central-and-Southern Pacific and Texas-and-Pacific had terminals in San Francisco. They tried their hardest to put each other out of business by slashing passenger rates until they reached ridiculously low figures.

Collis P. Huntington controlled the Central-and-Southern. Colonel Thomas A. Scott of the Pennsylvania Railroad was interested in the Texas-and-Pacific. Huntington's passion for old masters and private libraries is well remembered. I know very little about Colonel Scott's acquisitive tastes, but it has always pleased my fancy to think of him as also being some sort of collector, if only of match-boxes or cigar-humidors. This was necessary to complete my picture of the railroad rate war as a struggle between match-boxes and paintings for the balance of power. The rate war had an important bearing upon my future, and I wanted to simplify the principles of the contestants for the sake of the stories I expected to tell my grandchildren. These grandmother stories have a traditional form. "Granny, won't you tell us about your romance with grandpa?" "Well, little dears, it all happened because of the new style shoe-buckle they were wearing in the year 1662. You see, children, as I was walking down the street."

Collectors' aims and grannies aside, the rate war had a broadening effect upon San Franciscans. With railroad rates so cheap, why not travel? Why stay at home, even though "home" was the finest State on God's green earth, etc. The railroads did everything but pay people to travel. San Francisco acquired the disappearing habit. If someone was missing between breakfast and lunch, it was assumed that he had been inveigled into making the trip to New York. Each succeeding day the number of friends and acquaintances one saw upon the street lessened. "Cut-rate" tickets was a certain explanation.

One day my father came home with an excursion round-trip ticket for New York. He was to have his first vacation in years. Thanks to the rate war, which enabled him to travel both ways for fifty dollars, he could go East, visit Richmond, and enjoy the company of some of the scholars with whom he had been corresponding. It was this correspondence, he often said, which helped him over the rough places of his rabbinate in the West.

Father was not the only one to take a vacation. Though on the whole robust, I had suffered ill health for several months, and the family physician had prescribed an ocean voyage. So it was decided that I should sail to Panama, visit my brother Felix there, then cross the Isthmus, and board an Atlantic vessel for New York. The thought of such a voyage, to be followed by a trip to Richmond, reconciled me to illness. One week after my father left by rail, I sailed on the Colima, the very steamship aboard which my brother had served as physician after leaving medical school.

The day before I sailed a certain young San Franciscan who had showed a liking for me broached the subject of marriage. He wanted me to engage myself to him, and marry upon my return. Though he importuned me to say "Yes," I determined not to commit myself until my return to San Francisco. To rest and regain strength were my only immediate concern. And I wanted to have the pleasure of travelling without a thought of this responsibility awaiting me when I got back.

These, I realize, were but surface objections; had they not sufficed, I might have found others. It was a career of service I was dreaming of, rather than a life limited to housewifely duties. Since early high-school days, when Mary Kincaid had shown me the way back to my people, my thoughts and acts had been influenced by the desire to do some useful and significant work.

The passage to Panama was delightful. We touched at many little Mexican ports en route. Going ashore, I had glimpses of an alien civilization. And there were surprises. My beloved brother had arranged with Pacific Mail representatives in each seaport to meet me with letters and gifts. Small wonder that, with the balmy air, the picturesque places of call, the brotherly greetings, and a short trip to beautiful Mexico City, I was a changed person when I arrived at Panama.

My brother in his professional environment was not the care-free fellow who had trudged the hills of San Francisco with me in our school days. He had many responsibilities; was charged with administrative duties usually entrusted to men twice his age. Phenomenal his rise!

Meeting him after months of separation was a joyful event, but the information he gave me was the greatest surprise of all. My father had written him that he had accepted a call from a Baltimore congregation, and that the family would soon move East. And in New York he had made the acquaintance of the great Alexander Kohut and his family, had even become an intimate friend of his; the two were almost inseparable. I was to meet them both upon my arrival.

Joyful tidings, this Baltimore call! My brother was disappointed to see me so enthusiastic.

New York

For the moment I forgot that it meant permanent separation from him, from my oldest sister and from my brother Paul. Felix loved the West coast, and hoped to return to California some day and establish a practice. And here we were planning to put the continent between us, and I was cheerful about it. It was a saddened brother who conducted me on a tour of inspection, showing me the great cuts and the monster dredges at work on the De Lesseps undertaking.

Only a few hours with him, then I crossed the Isthmus and embarked for New York.

Human, all too human, is our trait of turning from that which is dear to us, without thought. All my friends and associations were of San Francisco. I had grown up there. It was the place of my memories, a city beautiful and picturesque, a city with a soul. Yet I could think only of the glorious and inspiring future that the East offered.

My father met Alexander Kohut at a time when the latter was in a state of extreme depression. In his one year in the United States, much had happened to envelop his home in sadness.

The serious illness of his wife was one of the reasons why he had come to the United States. The physician who had been attending her, and in whom they felt complete confidence, had migrated to this country.

Another reason was the great literary venture in which he had been engaged for twenty years.

Twelve to fourteen hours a day was the time he always devoted to the *Aruch Completum*. Philosophers, European academies of science, Hebraists and Orientalists recognized its epoch-making value even in its early stages of publication, and encouraged him in whatever way they could. The publication of each successive volume, however, represented untold struggles. Sufficiently arduous was the labor of preparation; but the task of securing publication, the promises, disappointments, rebuffs, worst of all, the indifference to Jewish scholarship of men famous as Jewish Mæcenases, would have broken a lesser man. Volume by volume it appeared, as though wrung from his blood and soul. And as each volume meant a recurrence of the same difficulties in securing financial support, he was in despair.

Then America appeared on his horizon. The death of Adolph Huebsch, the brilliant New York rabbi who wrote the most beautiful prayer book I have seen, left an important pulpit vacant; and his congregation decided to fill his place with another European rabbi, preferably a scholar of distinction. The rabbinate was offered to Alexander Kohut, who deliberated a long time before accepting it. As chief rabbi at Grosswardein, presiding over a number of congregations, and as Jewish representative-elect in the Hungarian parliament, he seemed permanently bound to the life of Hungary. But constant suasion to bring him to America was being exerted upon him, and he was finally led to make the decision by the combination of his wife's illness, increased difficulties in publishing the *Aruch*, and political and Jewish conditions in Hungary.

Though Hungary was loath to see him go, yet his decision once made, his congregants and colleagues made of his departure a state occasion, with torchlight processions.

He came to America with no thought of entering into controversy; rather, with a spirit of deep religious sentiment. Polemics were never to his taste. Yet suddenly he found himself pitchforked into a dispute with Dr. Kohler, a dispute not of his seeking. His wife was ill, his eight children were in a strange environment, afraid of America and Americans. They pleaded to be taken back to Hungary. And under such conditions he was called upon to be the standard-bearer of historical Judaism. He accepted the duty and acquitted himself nobly. But his life was saddened by the death of his wife. In America his children learned their first lessons in suffering.

When my father came to New York, he attended one of Dr. Kohut's sermons and later introduced himself. Here was a Hungarian, a colleague, one of the first subscribers to the *Aruch Completum*; Alexander Kohut took him to his heart. There was an immediate bond. My father, too, had known the sadness of losing a dear one, of caring for motherless children. His human qualities buoyed up Dr. Kohut considerably. In an incredibly short time—no more than a few hours—they were as intimate as if they had been lifelong friends. Father spent the remainder of his stay in New York under the Kohut roof, immersed himself in all the newcomer's American problems, made friends with the children, and by his magnetism lifted the entire family from its despondency.

The California rabbi who came to New York for a vacation forgot the vacation completely. A week went by, and he did none of the things he had planned on the way East. His time was soon up, and he had to return to California immediately, or forfeit his cut-rate ticket. On the whole, though, it was an eventful trip—he had found a new rabbinate and made a new friend.

A week after he left New York, I arrived. The ocean voyage had had the expected results. My cough was gone, and I was very much alive and eager for what was to come next. On leaving Panama I had been delighted with the thought of living in the East. But as the ship progressed, and as the beauty of California at a distance enhanced itself tenfold in my inner vision, my spirits drooped.

However, the first sight of New York lifted me out of myself. The skyline! In 1886 the New York skyline did not boast towering monuments to life insurance, sewing-machines and five-and-ten-cent stores. None the less it was impressive enough to stir one's emotions and make one feel strange powers. I do not believe there was ever a time when New York from the harbor was not an imposing sight.

My home while in New York was to be with a cousin. She was waiting at the pier when the ship arrived, also a boyhood friend of Felix's. On the way to East Fifty-first Street she told me that three or four times during the preceding days Dr. Kohut's daughters had called to inquire about my arrival. My father, I learned, had told them about me and my intending to stay in New York, and had asked them to make friends with me.

At my cousin's house I had no more than exchanged greetings with the rest of my relatives when the door-bell rang. Three unusual persons entered, two of them tall, beautiful young women of about nineteen and eighteen, who approached me with smiling faces and arms extended. Following them was a man, seemingly their older brother, who was the most remarkable looking individual I had ever seen. Over six feet in height, a commanding and dramatic figure with very white skin and blue-black hair, there was something about his face which aroused one's interest and curiosity, something of the outer and inner world in the strong, regular features and the flashing, magnetic eyes, which seemed to be both introspective and penetrating.

Soon I learned that the three were not brother and sisters, but father and daughters; they were the Kohut girls and Alexander Kohut. On their way home from synagogue services they had decided to ask about me again and had been delighted to learn that I had arrived. They stayed only a few minutes, long enough, however, to arrange for another meeting in the afternoon and a walk through Central Park.

In those few minutes I felt I had acquired friends who would always be my friends. We often grope for years, uncertain of our ways; suddenly a spark is struck and we know instinctively that this is the great thing we have been looking and longing for.

I broke an appointment for the same afternoon, with friends made aboard the ship, and met the Kohuts again.

During our long walk together I was in a state of continual amazement at these people who were unlike any I had known before. Dr. Kohut was twenty years older than his oldest daughter, but his relation to his children was like a brother's. He never exercised parental authority as I had seen it in my own home, where there was always a certain distance between ourselves and our parents. This tall man who struggled to express himself in English seemed in certain respects never to have grown up.

My impression of him that afternoon was that he was a man to whom every hour of life was important, be it for work or for play. He enjoyed the air he breathed, gave unsuspected significance to seemingly trivial things in the conversation,

New York

and through his questioning and comments made me realize more about myself than I had ascertained through all the years of introspection in which I had indulged. Amazingly enough, this light shone through the fog of his awkward English. He struggled and struggled for the expression of an idea, and sighed with relief when he succeeded finally in making himself clear. He explained that he had full command, colloquial and in writing, of Hebrew, Hungarian, German, French, Italian and Latin. "Yet here I am, struggling with English, as if I had been dumb all my life."

During the walk he related an incident of his arrival in the United States. A newspaper reporter had asked him for a "story." You may say," Dr. Kohut replied, "that a millionaire rabbi has arrived." "How do you come by your wealth?" the reporter asked. "My children are worth at least a million dollars to me, and my library another million." The reporter left disgusted.

I returned to my cousin's home in time for dinner. That evening, for the third time in the one day, the Kohuts and myself met, the father, the two daughters, the oldest son, a dreamy-eyed boy of twelve who was in many respects a copy of his father. Dr. Kohut brought me a book, a novel then attracting a good deal of attention because it was the first story dealing with Jewish life in New York. Moreover it was written by a non-Jew. Few persons of this generation have read or heard of *The Yoke of the Torah*, by Sidney Luska (pen-name of Henry Harland). For a season in the eighties it was a much-discussed book, then went the way of all ephemera. It had a special significance for Dr. Kohut, however; it was the first book in English which he read from cover to cover—an achievement, the result of intense perseverance and continual reference to a German-English dictionary, but holding a sweet savor for him. He enjoyed the story so much that on his daily walk he usually headed for Beekman Place, the quiet little street above the East River at Fifty-First Street that was the locale of the story. The author lived there and had described as the home of the heroine an actual house, the corner dwelling. For that house Dr. Kohut developed a romantic attachment. It was not just a structure of brick and brown-stone, but a place of dreams and the spirit. Henry Harland had given the house a soul.

All these things Dr. Kohut told me when he presented the book. He ended by saying he hoped I would find the story as interesting as he had.

The conversation then turned upon my father's expectations and the family in San Francisco. In the week that he had spent under the Kohut roof he had spoken very proudly and in detail of his children, and I was amazed to find that the Kohuts knew all about us, knew our names and our traits and ambitions, knew of Felix's medical activities, my sister's contralto, my own keen interest in women's rights and things Jewish. My father had even spoken to this new-found friend about my absorption in the Kohut-Kohler controversy, and of my being wrought up over the fact that Dr. Kohler had assailed Alexander Kohut so soon after his arrival, putting him in an uncomfortable position in a strange land.

The Kohuts were delighted that our family was to settle in the East, for through my father and myself they already felt a spirit of love and kinship. When they left that evening, I looked back upon the events of the day—my first in New York. Wonderful, they seemed. Not that I had seen much of the great city, but I had met several rare human beings.

My father had left word with my cousins that I was not to return but to await the family's removal to Baltimore. The length of my stay in New York was dependent upon the time of their arrival. In the interim I was to visit Richmond, fulfilling a long-expressed wish.

I was truly my father's daughter. He had come to New York for a vacation, and after meeting the Kohuts had shelved all his plans. And here was I. Visits, shopping, theatres, sight-seeing —all the activities young women dream about when planning a trip to New York, all the diversified amusements and educational expeditions that were going to take up every minute of my time— where were they? The things I had planned to do seemed of little importance. The friends I made on the steamship I never saw again, though we had arranged to have many meetings in New York.

A week after my arrival in New York a conference of Jewish ministers was held in Temple Emanu-El. Most of the personages about whom I had read so much while in San Francisco were to be present. An open meeting was scheduled at which Dr. Kohut was to deliver an address; his subject, "The Conflict Between Science and Religion." Much depended upon the effect of his speech upon his listeners, for he was to state his case to his opponents as well as to his adherents. The outcome might be a continuation or extension of the theological war, or it might be the first move towards a rapprochement, with moderation in both camps as a result.

I attended with the Kohut girls. It was interesting to see all those rabbis of conflicting beliefs gathered in one assemblage, listening to their respective opponents. Face to face, people cannot hate each other as much as if either side recedes into a vague symbol of menace. Here were these men, leaders all, who had to state their viewpoint for their opponents. No flights of rhetoric, no appeals to lay prejudices and passions, no beclouding the issues were possible if these men were really sincere in their desire to arrive at amity.

So many rabbis were present at Temple Emanu-El that it seemed there could have been none left anywhere else. As we entered the Temple I was introduced to my father's dear friend, Benjamin Szold, to Kaufmann Kohler, to Bernhard Felsenthal, to the lovable Gustav Gottheil, and Aaron Wise, father of Rabbi Stephen S. Wise, the man of vision who sought to bring opponents together on common ground, and to many other men whose names stood for living beings with me because of our conversations and readings at home.

Dr. Kohut being the storm centre of the conflict between Orthodoxy and Reform, and his address being a statement of his position, there was intense eagerness in the audience—but none more eager than myself. I experienced a strange, unaccountable feeling of nervousness, a fear that through some unforeseen misfortune the address might not prove a success. More than anything else in the world, I wished that this remarkable man should prevail.

When the applause came, I was happy. I remember with what gratification I saw Dr. Kohler rush forward and congratulate his antagonist. My feeling of resentment against Dr. Kohler for his early attacks vanished, and I realized how much my father missed in San Francisco through not being associated with men who could submerge the momentary controversy and meet each other with generosity.

We left the Temple an excited, chattering group, and walked north on Fifth Avenue. As we parted at Fifty-first Street I could not resist telling Dr. Kohut how proud I was of him and of his friendship, and how happy I was that he had triumphed. His only answer was a pressure of his hand on mine.

That evening my cousin and I sat at home exchanging confidences. When two young women wax confidential, need one inquire the subject? When it became my turn to unveil the secrets of my heart I began by relating incidents from some of my romances and describing young men and their ways as I knew them, but ended abruptly: "I know now why I have never given my heart to anyone. Only a man like Alexander Kohut could have an appeal for me."

My cousin could not resist the temptation to titter.

"What are you laughing at?" I demanded hotly.

"I wasn't laughing," she said, haltingly. "I was just thinking—he has eight children."

"It wouldn't make any difference to me if he had eighty," I cried.

Chapter vii

"SO GREAT A DECISION"

THE following days went by only too rapidly. Though I made plans to go to Richmond, I could hardly tear myself away from New York. Yet finally I did go.

The evening before my departure I dined at the Kohut home, the first and only time during my stay in New York. Here I met all the children, Gisela, tall and beautiful, with brown hair and blue eyes; Helen, with raven hair and her father's brown eyes and wearing a big bunch of keys hooked into her belt in real old European *Hausfrau* style; George, a thoughtful lad of twelve; Valerie, erratic and temperamental, whose mission, it seemed, was to care for her father's physical wants; Margaret, nicknamed by the children "Santa Marghareta" because of her piety and angelic disposition; Louis and Eugene, who looked like twins, although they were two years apart; and Elizabeth, the "after-thought," who was so much younger than the others. Though everything in the house seemed colored black because of the mourning attire, there was a radiance of love and devotion permeating the home that can never be effaced from my memory.

After dinner Dr. Kohut invited me to look at his "million-dollar library." He showed me valuable books "worth their weight in gold" and precious manuscripts in the languages of the East, dating from the sixteenth century. So fine a library in the possession of an individual I had not seen before. My enthusiasm led him to show me all his treasures. As he spoke, the room seemed peopled with great shades.

"We have aired our opinions of them," he said, indicating the books, "but what do they think of us? What will this generation contribute that is worthy to stand on the same shelves with them? We must be humble and we must toil very hard. And we must have encouragement and sympathy so that we do not falter." He looked up quickly, and fixed his gaze intently upon me. "My daughters love you. They worship you. They have hopes that some day you will come into their home as their mother. And I . . . I am more anxious than they . . . will you be my wife?"

The transition from the reflective to the extremely personal was so sudden that for a moment I did not know what to say. But in the next moment I found myself answering in a quiet, even tone—to my own amazement—that I, too, had been thinking about it, and while I would give him no answer until my family came East, I felt that fate had brought our families together

"So Great a Decision"

and that possibly my life's work was to serve him and his children.

Like every other young woman, I had often imagined the grand heroics which tradition associates with romantic scenes. Yet here the moment had come, and it had been very quiet and direct for both of us, and—satisfactory. I asked Dr. Kohut, however, not to mention the subject again until I was once more under my father's roof.

The next day I telegraphed the news to my father, and also cabled Felix at Panama. By return wire I received a stern rebuke from my father, who ordered me to leave New York at once. Messages began coming in in batches, and all to the same effect. My oldest sister, who had mothered me, was heart-broken to think of the awful fate that might befall me. My father wired me not to commit myself in any way. My dear little stepmother, who had herself married a widower with six children, registered herself by wire as being against my "foolishness."

I did not see Dr. Kohut again before I left New York. He sent me a note at my cousin's home, enclosing a letter which he asked me not to open until I stood beside my mother's grave in Richmond. Naturally, I was eager to know what the letter contained, and curious as to his purpose in making such an unusual request.

The first day of my stay in Richmond I visited the Jewish cemetery, where as a child I had spent so many "happy hours." It was rapidly growing dark. But the flames from the foundry in the ravine below threw their glow as of old over the hillside. I stood at my mother's grave and opened the letter. It was a prayer to the Almighty that I receive guidance in making so great a decision. In tears I read it aloud.

Several days later, while I was gradually becoming familiar again with Richmond and its people, I received a cable from Felix expressing faith in my judgment and assuring me of his support should I decide to marry Dr. Kohut. It gladdened me, of course, that at least one member of my family did not disapprove, but I could not understand why Felix, so many thousands of miles away, and possessing meagre information, should express himself upon the outcome with such confidence. It seemed strange. The most worldly of us all, he had in his younger days taken a decided stand against the rabbinate. He hated poverty and knew that a rabbi's family faced a continual material struggle. Yet for me he advocated marriage with a rabbi, and with a rabbi whom he knew to be so much older than myself, and a man with a family of eight children.

In a letter that followed about a week later came the explanation. Felix wrote that from what he knew of my character and desires, association with such a wonderful man would more than make up for things that in marriage with an ordinary man would be unthinkable. The time had come to face realities, he said, and the realities in my case were that I was not worldly, and would most likely be very unhappy married to a man who could only provide material blessings. He felt that to one with my viewpoint there should be no real obstacle to the marriage.

This letter shed a new light upon Felix. In my correspondence with my family, I informed them of my determination, but added that I did not want to marry without their consent. All of them sent me letters in opposition. I was kept busy answering their contentions and disarming their skepticism. My little stepmother was perhaps more vehemently opposed than any other member of the family. She loved us all too much to be ready to allow any of us to assume a life of care and responsibility as against one of ease and comfort.

Despite all the skepticism and warnings, I refused to be frightened. Very true it is that "nothing is bad but thinking makes it so."

From Richmond my destination was Baltimore, where I was to await the coming of the family. I made my home with the family of my father's colleague and lifelong friend, Benjamin Szold.

I found myself in a shelter, like our own home in San Francisco, noted for its hospitality to rich and poor of any color or creed. The very house, on Lombard Street, one of the oldest sections of the city, suggested hospitality, in its fine square rooms, cheerful, informal furnishings, and garden in the rear tended by the entire family, including the rabbi himself, who rose on summer mornings at five o'clock to dig, or prune, or weed, or merely meditate before sitting down to his scholar's desk.

His serene study, or library, lined with fine oak bookcases rising to the ceiling seemed like a replica of our own in San Francisco; and I spent many a solitary hour there, at night, when none of the family were about, browsing among the books. It was in that room that Dr. Szold wrote his monumental book, a commentary in Hebrew—which language he wielded like his native tongue—on the Book of Job.

Dr. Szold, a handsome man with mild, brown eyes in a fine-featured olive face, was one of those simple, saint-like persons who will give the coat off their backs to a beggar on the street. Cardinal Gibbons once said of him in a conference of ministers of all sects at which he was present: "Here is the best Christian in the room."

Sometimes too Christ-like for his more practical wife, who had to save the pennies so that her five daughters might be educated. Mrs. Szold was a type rather rare among Jews in those days. She always suggested the soil—a hearty life of plenty in a flourishing farmstead. Such, in Hungary, as a matter of fact, had been her home. And it was as if some peasant blood had entered her veins and made the blue of her eyes and the roses in her cheeks and given her the gift to be a most delicious cook and expert needlewoman. She

"So Great a Decision"

passed on to some of her children a veritable passion for the earth and animals and all outdoor things.

So it was a real home I had that summer. Henrietta, the oldest daughter, the intellectual one, her father's adorer and adored, now a leading Zionist, founder of the international Zionist organization of women, became my lifelong friend. Rachel, the second daughter, sitting under the grape arbor in the garden playing the guitar and singing, seemed the most beautiful creature in the world. I believe she *was* considered the loveliest Jewish girl in Baltimore. All the Szolds helped me in my efforts to find a home and furnish it.

But we never discussed my romance. Later, however, I was told that I talked about it in my sleep.

In September my father came, alone, to Baltimore. He asked me whether I was certain I wanted to go through with the marriage; whether I was fully aware of the trials and difficulties ahead. Again I stated my case; it didn't seem a difficult task. I had a stepmother and knew a stepmother's problems. My stepmother was an invalid, while I was strong and in perfect health. I had lived in a rabbi's home and knew a rabbi's problems. I was a rabbi's child and knew the difficulties besetting the paths of rabbi's children. It was to be a career for me and, as I regarded things, a successful career.

Father communicated with New York. Two days later I went with him to Philadelphia, where Dr. Kohut came to meet us. Happy the day for the two of us. We were formally engaged, though not to marry for many months.

We laid plans for exchange of letters. We would write each other not only as friends, but also as teacher and pupil. He was to enclose exercises in English, prepared by both himself and his children; I was to correct and return them. Little did I think, when I received my teacher's diploma from the normal school of San Francisco, that my first pupils would be my future husband and his children.

Nor did the obligation to study rest wholly with him. I began the study of German, the language in which he preached. We laughingly agreed that he was to marry the English language and I the German language. I hoped to be of service to him in translating his sermons and lectures for English publication; perhaps also some of his earlier books.

Our Baltimore home soon became a meeting-place for Jewish students of the Johns Hopkins University, and a young student who spoke broken English agreed to direct my German speech if I could correct his English. Thus I made rapid progress. I devoted myself to the reading of Lessing, Heine and Goethe, and while in New York my fiancé delved into Emerson and American history and familiarized himself with the geography of the country.

My father assumed his duties as rabbi of the First Baltimore Hebrew Congregation. From an apathetic congregation it soon developed under his influence into one of the prides of the community, flourishing as never before. Within a few years its building in Lloyd Street became inadequate, and a new house of worship was decided upon which would be commodious and a thing of beauty. Characteristically, my father made many new friends and became identified with communal activities. He was able to continue more intimately his friendship of fourteen years' standing with Cardinal Gibbons, who was now permanently established in Baltimore. Another interesting friendship was that with Dr. Gilman, President of Johns Hopkins University. Mary Wilson, a rare human being of great literary ability, joined a number of other Christians in studying Hebrew at our home under my father's direction. We have a noble, impassioned poem in his memory from her pen.

When the rest of the family came from San Francisco a few weeks after my father's arrival, I gloated over what I considered a personal triumph. Without previous housekeeping experience, I had rented a house, furnished it completely, and had a hot meal waiting upon the table when the family crossed the threshold. In accepting the congratulations of the new arrivals upon a task well performed, I experienced a glow of satisfaction in the feeling that I was thus preparing myself for my future duties.

Baltimore, with its streets and streets of red brick houses with low flights of white marble steps—the degree of whiteness indicative of good or bad housekeeping—was in marked contrast to San Francisco. Frisco the hustling, Baltimore the conservative—perhaps the most conservative city in the United States. San Franciscans revelled in the beauty of their city, while Baltimoreans, with a touch of aristocracy, took themselves and their city for granted. Here was no picturesque Ah Sing, the faithful family cook, trotting off to market with the basket upon his shoulder. Men and women of means—the bluest of social bluebloods—carried their own baskets. The practice does not obtain today.

For the first few days the new arrivals said very little about my prospective marriage. Doubt still remained, however, with my stepmother; and not only doubt, but antagonism. My younger sister Cyd was outspoken in her grief over what she called my deliberate sacrifice. The opposition of these two and the implied though unvoiced disapproval of the others made the first few weeks of our resumed family life rather unhappy. I busied myself with correspondence and study, and filled in time by teaching the congregation's religious school. Except for the Szolds I made no friends in Baltimore, regarding the city as only a temporary dwelling-place.

The years of 1885-6-7 may be regarded as perhaps the most important in the development of Judaism in the United States. As a young woman who had only recently evolved from an apathetic, indeed antagonistic Jewess, to one who was full of the spirit of religion, I became very bitter against the rabbis who were themselves unholy and irreligious in that they devoted themselves to attacking other rabbis in preference to promoting spiritual worship among their own congregants. Most of the ministers, as I saw them, were vainglorious. One minister was arrayed against another just as one congregation competed with another. Congregations, I felt, should be endowed. No more should be established than a community could sustain. One well-supported congregation with three rabbis—dividing the activities of social welfare, worship and education—was better, in my opinion, than three congregations poorly maintained, poorly equipped, and providing the letter rather than the spirit.

It was my oft-reiterated opinion that the time would come when a division of congregational duties would be necessary for rabbis, and that rabbis should be trained so that some could devote themselves exclusively to philanthropic and social programs, while others gave their entire consideration to research work and the fostering of

Jewish scholarship. I believe in fewer synagogues, with more rabbis attached to them, as in other churches. I think this was the vision Isaac M. Wise had when he organized the Hebrew Union College.

Isaac M. Wise was not a great scholar in the European sense. Perhaps it was because he lived and worked in a time when American Jewry needed a constructive congregational and social program rather than the exclusive development of Jewish science and literature. But I believe that no one, regardless of which branch of Judaism he prefers, will deny to Dr. Wise a first place in the history of Jewish congregational life in this country.

I hold the view that ministers should be appointed for life. This would do away with the humiliating experiences of elections, at which rabbi after rabbi is invited to preach a trial sermon, so that the congregation could decide between a rising inflexion or a reverberating basso, without regard to the rabbi's spiritual qualities.

My father, upon being invited once to preach a trial sermon, said: "I am not a prize horse to be led out for either admiration or purchase."

More than ever I informed myself of all that was going on in American Jewry. The Pittsburgh conference, with its "Declaration of Independence" directed principally against Dr. Kohut, had reacted beneficially upon Orthodoxy through the establishment of the Jewish Theological Semi-

"So Great a Decision" 115

nary. The association of Sabato Morais and Alexander Kohut at this time was a very happy one. The organization of an Orthodox Seminary had been in Dr. Morais's thoughts for a number of years. Dr. Kohut, too, had dreamed of such a seminary. He saw it as one modeled upon the great Breslau Seminary, where he had studied under Graetz and Frankel. The time was propitious, friends came forward, the Seminary was founded. Dr. Morais was for calling it the Orthodox Seminary. Dr. Kohut, who was tired of doctrinal dissension, who even dreamed of bringing all the factions together into one universal house of worship, held that a general name like Jewish Theological Seminary was preferable. Sabato Morais was its first president, and Alexander Kohut occupied the Talmudic Chair.

Thus one of the great seats of learning, the training-place of many of the most distinguished leaders of today, the home of the greatest Jewish library in the world, owes its existence to the fevered controversy of the 1880s. The demand for a seminary gave rise to a further demand for an association to finance the publication of Jewish works. The Jewish Publication Society was formed, another outgrowth of the need that had been expressed in the founding of the seminary. Dr. Kohut was appointed to the publication committee.

Unpleasant were these years, but out of the strife came good.

A month before our marriage my fiancé sent me amazing news.

During one of his walks, after being up most of the night working upon the *Aruch Completum*, he had strolled, as he often did, over to Beekman Place to look at the street that had come to make such a strong appeal to his imagination.

This morning, however, there was something different about the corner house, No. 39. In the book no "For Sale" sign had appeared upon it. Now the notice dangled in the wind. Dr. Kohut went straight and hunted up the owner. The price asked was a staggering sum. Dr. Kohut's resources were half the amount. He gave what he had, and mortgaged himself for the rest.

So we were to commence our married life in our own home. And that home was to be the one in Beekman place figuring in *The Yoke of the Torah*.

He wrote me if I saw a beautiful, sad-faced girl upon the stairs, someone vaguely familiar, I must smile.

Real estate in New York has its divers aspects. Men buy it for speculation, for residences, for factories and offices, for investment. But to purchase real-estate because of a romance—that is rather by itself.

This was not the only instance of my husband's sentimentality. It manifested itself frequently throughout his life. His daughters, for example, were named after the princesses of the royal

"So Great a Decision" 117

family of Austro-Hungary. When the stock of princesses' names gave out, and there was another little Miss Kohut to be "christened," he chose the name of—a queen. His daughters were nothing less than princesses to him, and princesses' names they must have. Had his sons been born in the United States, no doubt they would have been named for Washington, Jefferson, Lincoln. But the naming of the girls would have been difficult. We must have a few women Presidents, if only to name our daughters after. Our only choice now is movie actresses. Mary Pickford is better known than Jane Addams, and how many know of Susan B. Anthony to each thousand who know of Gloria Swanson?

Chapter viii

MARRIAGE

IN FEBRUARY, 1887, we were married in Baltimore. The officiating rabbi was Benjamin Szold. It was a very small and none too cheery wedding group—*en famille*, except for Henrietta Szold, who enlivened what was a rather dismal ceremony by playing Mendelssohn's *Wedding March*.

The family's objections had given way to assent and acceptance of the inevitable. They had had almost a year in which to become inured to the idea, and had seen at every turn how imbued I was with the thought of spending myself in service, and in leading a life of significance. My oldest sister in far-off San Francisco was the most difficult to win over. Our "little mother" of the household loved with a love rare in even a sister. My assuming so great a responsibility appalled her, and my marriage seemed to her more like a funeral ceremony. As she told me later, the thought of my being immured within the walls of a home that was already filled with children seemed too terrible.

A few hours before the ceremony I wrote my

Marriage

sister: "I go to New York to be the wife of a great man and to become a mother to the motherless."

Yet with all my confidence and despite a year of preparation for the great work I was to undertake, certain misgivings came to me as we neared New York after the honeymoon. Success, I had felt, depended upon me alone, and if I did my share, all would be well. Suddenly now fear took possession. There were eight children awaiting me, eight individuals, each with a different temperament, soul, desires, likes and dislikes. They could not be viewed collectively; relations with each would have to be on an individual basis. I forgot, temporarily, the happy times I had enjoyed with them the year before; their eager eyes and smiling faces were blurred in my vision. In the grip of sudden fear, human beings do not appear to us clothed in all their human characteristics, but only as sharply accentuated symbols of the uneasiness in our own hearts. And so it was that for the moment I saw these charming children, with their delightful old world manners and their quaint Hungarian accent, with their naïve wonder at things American, as so many possibilities for misunderstandings.

How different the reality! My fears proved to be phantoms that plagued me for their own amusement; and I was ashamed of my momentary inability to resist their imputations. Such heart-warming greetings as I received when we arrived in New York were beyond my expectations. We started our life together, and continued it, in a spirit of mutual affection; and I felt that nothing could go wrong.

Motherless, in a strange land, called upon to adapt themselves to the life and customs of a new milieu, these children looked to me to guide them through the mazes. With delight I accepted the task. It was with no twinge of regret that I put aside, for the nonce, all thought of my own individuality and let myself be absorbed by the lives of my husband and children. This was what I had planned to do. I lived nine lives, not one after another, like the proverbial cat, but all at the same time.

A young woman who had known poverty as a rabbi's daughter did not expect opulence as a rabbi's wife. Pleasurable, though, was the knowledge that we had enough for our needs. My husband, dreamer and scholar, unable to count except upon his fingers, was nevertheless more practical and provident than my father. We had certain obligations that precluded indulgence in luxuries but there was no pressing problem of making both ends meet.

I was very ambitious for my children, and having discerned the promise of certain talents in several of them, was determined they should be encouraged. One or two of them loved music, and the organist of the congregation was engaged as their piano instructor. The rest having no such inclination, there was no reason why it should be

Marriage 121

forced upon them. Remembering my own abhorrence of piano practice, it was easy to decide that the Kohut exchequer should not be drained by drilling music into children to whom piano practice was a nightmare.

The inexperienced mother had determined that each of the boys and girls should have a profession, and even went so far as to say what profession. I wanted the second daughter, Helen, to be a physician, and the third, Margaret, to be a kindergarten teacher. Of the sons the oldest was to be a rabbi, the second a physician, the third a pharmacist. So that no time should be lost I took immediate steps to direct their studies along these lines.

My husband differed from me on most of the points in my programme, and would not agree to it, though he loved me for the spirit in which I had gone at it, and would have helped to carry it out, had he approved. The truth was, I was too inexperienced, and my ardor and emotions, however well-intentioned and devoted, were no adequate substitute for motherhood's steadily developed knowledge and intuitions.

The two blocks constituting Beekman Place were a little world in themselves. High up above the East River, and seemingly cut off from the rest of the city, the residents were very neighborly. All the houses were of the four-story brown-stone type, with high stoops. Their occupants, however they might don the inflexible mask of the proverbial New Yorker when away from home, were real human beings in Beekman Place. Within a week after my arrival, most of the neighbors called. My impression at that time was that some of them came not only from neighborliness but also from curiosity to see the young woman of twenty-two who had become the head of such a large family.

Across the street lived the family of Dr. Gaillard, editor of a medical journal; next to us Justice Harland and his son Henry Harland, author of *The Yoke of the Torah* and the best-seller of the nineties, *The Cardinal's Snuff Box*. The houses of Judge Cole and Surrogate Rollins were a few doors away. In these two blocks lived a number of musicians who have contributed much to the pleasure of the most music-blessed of American cities. On quiet summer evenings, when windows were open, we had the choice of listening to good violin playing, or to the tones of talented piano virtuosi, or to the singing of great artists. Sometimes, however, violin, piano and voice all went at once—the lyric soprano of Marie Gramm, leading singer of St. Thomas's Church, the piano and the violin of the Frankos—Nahan and Sam—both popular orchestra leaders, the fortissimo of Isidore Luckstone, talented composer, and the beautiful soprano of the girl who was the model for Sidney Luska's heroine. She afterwards went to Milan to continue her vocal studies. Another resident of Beekman Place was the famous German composer, Franz Xavier Scharwenka.

In the summer we sat either on our stoop or a neighbor's stoop for a friendly chat—a pleasant custom lost today to middle-class New Yorkers of the apartment house era.

Residence on our side of the street gave us an advantage which our opposite neighbors did not enjoy. We had another world to look out upon, a feast for eye and imagination. At any moment we might banish thought of the street, the neighbors, the city, and give ourselves over to the fascinating world of river sights. Our rear windows looked out upon the East River which flowed almost directly below. Twilight was our favorite hour for the view. Blackwell's Island, which by day stood as a double symbol of law and human tragedy, lost its sinister aspect as it merged with the dusk and became something fantastic. In the full light of midday it resembled some grim feudal fortress. With its lamps lit, the penitentiary suggested anything from a palace to an amusement casino. Lights that to the people there were illumination were for us provocateurs of the imagination. We looked forward to the first snowfall, which covered the harsh buildings with a white blanket of seeming tenderness; and spring announced itself by the green of the Virginia creepers covering its walls. Spring outside; winter inside.

The river craft slipped silently by, like mysterious, shadowy personalities. Noisy excursion boats, with bands playing, freighters bound for the Connecticut shore, vessels under sail. What a view to have from one's windows. That part of the city has been too little appreciated. In recent years, and a few blocks further north, it has revived in favor as a residential district. Elizabeth Marbury, Anne Morgan and their friends have made of Sutton Place, in the shadow of the Queensborough Bridge, a very charming colony, and created from their back windows a picture worthy of Whistler and Pennell.

As I write this, I learn that the brown-stone houses of Beekman Place—in recent years considerably run down—are to give way to a huge fashionable apartment house. The places dear to us will soon be no more.

My husband had so many friends and well-wishers that there was a constant stream of visitors at the house. His favorite room was his library, on the fourth floor of the house, where he toiled daily and nightly over the *Aruch Completum*. Here came his visitors, all classes and manner of men—congregants, scholars, philanthropists, Christian clergymen, even Reform adversaries. Isaac M. Wise was drawn to him personally. A frequent visitor was the philanthropist and Jewish champion, Jacob H. Schiff, ever my husband's and my friend. Dr. William Hayes Ward, editor of the Independent, was a familiar figure at the "fourth floor rear," as Dr. Kohut's associates jocularly termed his retreat. Dr. Charles Eaton came there on many occasions, as also Dr. S. S. MacArthur and Robert Collyer of Calvary Baptist Church. We often greeted Michael Heilprin, also a Hungarian, an ardent Zionist and co-editor of the American edition of the *Encyclopedia Britannica*, also Solomon Silberstein, the Neo-Spinozist; Michael Rodkinson, who translated the Talmud into English; Naphthali Herz Imber, celebrated Hebrew poet; Adolph Radin, Jewish chaplain at New York State's penal institutions; Arnold B. Ehrlich, the great Hebrew linguist, who taught George Kohut and Stephen S. Wise Hebrew.

There were certain visitors, the bane of every leader, who had no spiritual kinship with him and no real purpose in coming. They only imposed upon his time and hospitality, eccentrics of all kinds who came with their belongings and tried to camp in our abode indefinitely. It was before the days of organized philanthropy, when mendicants begged from door to door. They all headed for the rabbi's home, and insisted upon seeing him, and took of his time and money. Immigrant Jews, given his address by European rabbis, came to the house directly from the ship, and deposited their problems and their belongings with us. In later years the community developed institutions which care for them as a matter of course, but to us of an earlier decade they were a trying problem. The children and myself often expressed impatience with these uninvited guests who intruded upon a large and busy household, but the gentle and overindulgent host reproved us mildly.

Such prodigious toil as my husband devoted to the structure of the *Aruch Completum* was beyond all my preconceived ideas of his work. It was really the paramount motive of his career. During the Baltimore days when I looked forward to the problems of married life, I counted my future charges as a husband and eight children. Soon I learned I should have counted them as a husband, the *Aruch Completum*, and eight other children. The oldest daughter called the *Aruch* her oldest brother, and pretended to be jealous of it. Certainly it received all the consideration and preference of the traditional first-born. The rest of us at certain times felt our secondary importance.

Day in and day out, whatever the demands upon his time and energy, Alexander Kohut managed to devote from ten to twelve hours to his beloved work; this over a period of twenty years. When congregational duties had to come first, he stole time from sleep and relaxation.

His first year in America had been so trying and time-consuming that he now sought, by redoubling his efforts, to carry forward his work at greater strides. Dawn often found him still at his library table immersed in a world of his own —nay, in millions of worlds. He was a Marco Polo of philology, going on a trip more wonderful than that of Cyrano de Bergerac to the moon. He beheld war, soothsayers, the Chaldeans, the Assyrians, the Temple, Babylon, the Persians, Rome, the Inquisition, York, the Tartars; he traveled through the past upon the crafts of a dozen different languages, and he saw a long line of scholars from Hillel and Shammai through Gamaliel and Akiba down to modern times, disdaining ease and comfort and worldly possessions in their desire to keep alive the heritage of the Fathers, giving additional light and significance and beauty to their religion. Words to him were not shop-worn instruments of a single use, but virtual planets, with light and heat and relativity, with more facets than a king's jewels, and a history through the ages that would encompass a thick volume for each of them.

The previous volumes of the *Aruch* had been printed in Vienna, where Dr. Kohut had left a batch of manuscript with the Chief Rabbi Güdemann to be set up when he departed for the United States. This manuscript in Vienna he referred to as his own. He sent additional batches as fast as he could complete them. When proof sheets were due, there was always excitement in the house. The child who received the package from the post-office and delivered it into the hands of the waiting father was always rewarded with a bright twenty-five-cent piece. The *Aruch* could not complain of being received without due ceremony.

Never will I forget the gloom that settled upon the household when it was learned that the steamship Elba, the very vessel in which the family had come to America, had gone down in the North Sea. We mourned not only those who had suffered disaster, but also a block of manuscript that had been despatched to Vienna aboard that vessel. A complete rewriting had to be made.

The third daughter, Valerie, always brought bread and milk to the toiler in the library before she went to bed each night. And the oldest boy, George, was ever hovering in his father's vicinity —a veritable shadow waiting for an opportunity to hand him some required book or restore the many used volumes to their accustomed shelves.

My deep concern for George, who was a delicate lad of thirteen and spent too much time indoors lying upon the sofa or watching his father at work, almost landed him in prison once. I had urged him to go out in the street and learn to play baseball with the other boys. It was the first time he followed my advice that he fell into trouble. Out in the street a stray baseball rolled in his direction. He picked it up intending to throw it back to the boys to whom it belonged, and raised his arm for his first baseball heave, when suddenly he felt it pinioned, and found himself in the grip of a plain-clothes policeman, who took him into custody for violation of a city ordinance.

About fifty boys tramped behind the desperate criminal until he was haled before the bar of justice at the police court. I was informed, and hurried breathless to the Fifty-seventh Street Court, to find little George, flanked by two burly policemen, being questioned by the magistrate. He had just given his name as I entered, and the magistrate, recognizing me, winked and said severely to the boy: "You have committed a terrible crime. You have broken the law. But, worse than that, you have proved yourself to be a bad baseball player. It took you too long to throw the ball back." Then, dismissing the case, he delivered himself of some scathing comments concerning policemen, who, with crime all about them, devoted themselves to taking little boys into custody for the sake of swelling their records of arrests.

The incident brought home to me a realization of the conditions militating against a healthy outlet for growing children, and when the Playground Association commenced its movement for consideration of the needs of boys and girls, I was one of its most ardent supporters. It has since been recognized that children have a right to play in the open, and if the city will not provide space for the purpose, its officials must expect them to play where they can. The playground movement and the establishment of the children's court are the answers to the cry of the children of the eighties and nineties for a mere half chance from the community.

George and his brothers soon found four or five ideal playmates in the Gaillard boys, the wildest Indians of Beekman Place, real boys, always trying new schemes to make life interesting, and never caring how hideous they made the nights for their neighbors, who were always hearing accounts of their deviltries. Once, wishing to convert their play-room into a dark-room for the development of photograph negatives, they splashed the walls with ink. And one winter they went in exclusively for things Indian, constructed an Indian tent and a canoe, did Indian war dances and let out wild war whoops. The shouting and hammering taxed the neighbors' nerves and patience. But when spring arrived and the boys let the tent and the canoe down through the windows and the neighbors saw the fruits of their winter's labor, their resentment changed into admiration and approval. The clever boys were forgiven their nocturnal massacres of quietude.

A fine bond was established between Edwin Gaillard and George Kohut. Curiously enough, both served later as librarians. Once during the early years at Beekman Place, the two boys were down at the river's edge when George became deathly sick and collapsed. Edwin carried him on his back up the steep stairway of the cliff to Beekman Place and into our home.

Marriage

On Friday afternoons, as preparations went forward for the evening services, one felt the house charged with the festival spirit. The Saturday morning clothes were laid out for each member of the family, and there was much running to and fro. My husband would put away his manuscripts, return his books to their shelves, come downstairs, and prepare for the evening services at the Temple. His last act before leaving the house would be to write to his mother in Hungary, and on his way to the synagogue, he would always deposit the letter in the mail box at Fifty-fourth Street and Lexington Avenue, which he had always used when he lived at Fifty-seventh Street, and continued to use, walking many blocks out of his way, not only after he moved to Beekman Place, but even later when he lived on Seventy-second Street.

Friday evenings were set apart to be spent at home in an entirely different way from the rest of the week. Duties were all put aside. Our week-day dinners were always jolly, but immediately after they were over, we gathered again around the long dining-room table to hold school. I helped the children with their lessons, particularly with English, and when not besieged with questions from them devoted myself to translations of my husband's writings, and to letters home. On Friday evenings, however, the programme was entirely different. Upon our return from services we sang and got up impromptu theatricals, and very often danced. People were never invited to our hilarious Friday evenings, though often we entertained unexpected visitors.

In that period of my life I had little time, and really had little call, for social and communal work. I felt myself dedicated to my husband, home, and children. But one of our neighbors in Beekman Place, drew me from retirement, Mrs. Ralph Trautman, founder and president of the Women's Health Protective Association, which is still in existence and a civic force in health protection, though its original programme was only local, to protect Beekman Place from nuisances. Later it was instrumental, along with other organizations, in having the law passed regulating the collection of garbage at stated hours. The Association's initial cause for being was popular with all the residents of Beekman Place. We suffered from the odors that came from the slaughter houses at Forty-ninth Street and First Avenue —the one drawback to that section, otherwise so lovely and delightful. The Association was trying to bring pressure upon the city health authorities to have the slaughter houses cleaned up.

Mrs. Trautman asked me to take part in the work, and I became a member one week after I arrived in New York. A protest meeting was called in Steinway Hall, at which I made my debut as a public speaker. Next morning, to my surprise, my remarks against the city administration for taking no action against the slaughter houses and for permitting garbage to accumulate in the streets were the only ones reported in the newspapers. My husband, while rather proud that what I had said seemed worthy of quotation, was dubious of the wisdom of a public career for me. He felt that I had much to do at home, and was more or less jealous of any time I gave to others. However, I continued with the Association for a number of years until pressure of household and other duties became so great that I had to give them my undivided attention.

Chapter ix

EUROPE

IN THE second year of our marriage my husband became ill. His herculean labors were beginning to tell upon his powerful constitution, and he suffered pain. A trip to Europe, it was felt, might improve his health considerably. Besides, he could see his old friends, visit his mother, and expedite the printing of the *Aruch*. Our family physician, Dr. Isaac Adler, brother of Felix Adler, strongly recommended this trip, and suggested that, while abroad, my husband consult a noted Viennese specialist.

A European vacation for a rabbi was a new experience to the congregation. Rabbis three and four decades ago were not expected to require vacations of any length; some received none at all. In truth the vacation idea did not prevail to any extent among the people themselves. It is only in recent years that the necessity for play has become so widely recognized. The week-end trip as an institution was unknown. Golfing and automobile riding were not active competitors of the churches.

At any rate, my husband's request for a vacation was granted, though I think the congregation attributed the innovation to his American wife and looked rather unkindly upon our going.

Life in New York had been eventful. It had been an exceedingly busy time, but withal interesting; and under such conditions did not seem a burden. The fears of my family had proved unfounded. I was very happy and felt that my life was worth while. The marriage had in no sense proved a sacrifice.

And now this European trip offered a new experience. I had always had a passion for travel, for seeing new scenes. As a child geography had been a favorite study and to this day I gloat over the articles and pictures in the *National Geographic Magazine.*

We left on the City of Paris, first of the "ocean greyhounds" which was to make a record trip. There was much excitement aboard; large wagers were made upon the time of the run. We lived from noon to noon to find out what the twenty-four hours' previous run had been. And actually she made the journey from New York to Southampton in five days and a fraction, setting a new speed for transatlantic travel.

England ten years before had been the scene of one of my husband's saddest experiences. It was still vivid in his memory. When it happened, he had already published the first volume of the *Aruch*, had completed the second in manuscript, and was seeking aid for its printing. Funds for the first volume he had secured by selling everything he possessed; the second faced an uncertain future. The Royal Academy of Vienna, recognizing the value of the work, assisted him with a subvention of four hundred florins. For the rest, friends advised him to seek a wealthy patron. He was a scholar, serving the cause of knowledge passionately, but was unversed in attracting the purses of the rich to himself. His friends told him that patrons were his only hope: Baron De Hirsch in Paris and Sir Moses Montefiore in England were contributing large amounts to Jewish causes and would doubtless be glad to assist such a worthy undertaking.

Advised by English scholars to confer with Sir Moses Montefiore, he came to London. He was cordially received by the chief rabbi, Dr. Herman Adler, who gave him a letter of introduction to Sir Moses, to whom Dr. Kohut had decided to dedicate his second volume. Dr. Adolph Neubauer of Oxford came especially from the University to meet and escort him to the Ramsgate train. Arrived at Ramsgate, after what seemed an endless journey, he went to the home of Sir Moses' secretary, who, the chief rabbi had stated, was to accompany him to the Montefiore home and act as his interpreter. But the secretary, Dr. Loewe, having just undergone an operation, was incommunicado, and the Hungarian rabbi was directed to try Sir Moses himself.

Discouraged, cold and hungry—he had not

eaten that day—he arrived at the princely abode and presented his letter of introduction. Sir Moses, he was informed, could see no one that day. On top of that, his return trip had cost him nearly his life. Obliged to wait several hours in the dark for a train, he mistook the whistle of a locomotive going in the opposite direction for that of his own train. Hurrying forward, he fell down a steep embankment and almost under the wheels of the passing train. It was after midnight when, bruised, disheartened and weary, he arrived in London. The chief rabbi was moved to real sorrow and sympathy when he heard the next day what happened, and offered to give the matter his personal attention, but Dr. Kohut made no further effort at that time to seek a patron in England.

In after years the author of *Aruch* realized of how little importance was his own work beside the monumental contributions of Sir Moses Montefiore to the Jewish cause. His own disappointment did not dim in his eyes the glory of the great Jew of Ramsgate, who made the supreme contribution to his people by his many pilgrimages to Palestine and his devotion to Jewish problems. Truly was Sir Moses the international philanthropist. When his centenary was celebrated the world over, the man he had refused financial aid for his literary undertaking was happy to raise his voice in the pulpit in praise of the great benefactor.

By the time he and I took our trip to London

together there had been a marked change in the fortunes of Alexander Kohut. No longer was he the unknown Hungarian seeking a patron, but the eminent scholar whose achievements had won him distinction in all the countries of Europe, and whom the New World had called to become one of its spiritual leaders. Historians like Ernest Renan and Heinrich Graetz, Orientalists like Max Müller, had acclaimed his work in superlative terms. The Imperial Academy of Science in Vienna, the Royal Hungarian Academy of Science in Budapest, the Cultus-Ministerium in Berlin had given him subventions and other assistance. Hungary had appointed him to its national parliament, leaders in Jewry like Jacob H. Schiff were deeply interested in his work. And Sir Moses' nephew, Claude Montefiore, the new head of the house, welcomed him warmly.

Our first day in London bade fair to be as dreary as my husband's visit to Ramsgate had been ten years before. Again the trouble was his dearest child, the *Aruch*. He had written the printer to send the last batch of proofs to the Royal Hotel in advance of our arrival. We found them there, and Dr. Kohut looked them over in our room. Then we went out with Dr. Schechter, and when we came back they were gone. Dr. Schechter helped us hunt, the hotel manager and many of the employees helped us hunt. Where could the proofs be? Had they gone down with the trash, or had some spy assumed they were papers of state importance and carried them off? Certainly the spectacle of the mad search and of our anxious faces provided a perfect setting for an E. Phillips Oppenheim story of international intrigue. No one surely could be so concerned about a few papers unless they were very secret, highly inflammatory, and contained plans against the safety of nations. Dr. Kohut would have made an ideal conspirator; he was tall, dark, handsome, foreign, and wore a Prince Albert coat. Suddenly a thought struck me. We went down to the laundry and rescued our precious proofs as they were about to be thrown into the vat of boiling soap water along with the soiled linen of our room.

My husband's main purpose in London was to meet the great Solomon Schechter, then Reader in Rabbinics at Cambridge, a chair founded for him by Claude Montefiore, and invite Professor Schechter to come to America as the head of the faculty of the Jewish Theological Seminary, as arranged by Sabato Morais, Jacob H. Schiff, and himself. It was at that time a struggling institution, and it was felt that the acquisition of so distinguished a personage as Solomon Schechter would serve to place the Seminary upon a firm footing. After a conference between Claude Montefiore, Professor Schechter, and Dr. Kohut, it was decided that the time was not yet ripe for Schechter to leave England. A number of years later, however, he did come to the United States and assumed the presidency of the Seminary.

Before he came to us at our hotel the first day, he had invited us to his Cambridge home, and we were about to start when we received a wire: "Don't come to Cambridge. Matilda has no cook." Not knowing Schechter, I was for the moment resentful, but who, knowing Schechter, as I did later, could really resent anything he did? Whatever he did, even a brutal insult, was a Schechterism, and one not only forgave but loved him for it. He was a Johnsonian sort of figure, and it is a pity he has had no Boswell to record all his clever, witty, brilliant, sometimes boyishly naughty sayings, or describe the causeries in his home, with "Matilda," the perfect hostess, smiling indulgently at her big child's roaring sallies. You felt that perhaps Schechter was luckier in his Matilda than Johnson in his Boswell. He needed someone to keep him in order without his knowing it—someone, metaphorically speaking, who would kindly let him get soup stains all over his waistcoat and not chide him for it, but who would see to it that in time they were cleaned away. Schechter was a different type from most of the Jewish scholars, more like a purely literary man. In fact, he was an omnivorous reader of current books, which he always managed to beg or borrow from friends. With his long beard and Jovian brow, he had a head for a portrait painter.

In the wake of the telegram Professor Schechter himself appeared at our hotel on the London embankment. "Ah, my dear friends, Cambridge without a cook is a tragedy! I will show you London instead."

I was delighted. Would he take us to see the Wallace collection, the Royal Gallery? The Tower? The Abbey? Kensington Gardens? And, of course, to my husband's objective, the British Museum? "Don't worry," he assured me, "you will see everything."

The three of us started out, I in the keenest of sightseeing moods. Directly the two commenced a discussion of some Hebrew text; their eyes shone, their faces glowed. Sightseeing, indeed! They were three or four thousand miles away, and as many years. London hadn't been built yet. There was no Tower, no Royal Gallery, no Baedeker; perhaps even no five o'clock tea. Those scholars! We tramped miles and miles without thought of direction, the one enkindled by the other's enthusiasm and magnetism; and the afternoon which was to acquaint me with the landmarks of English history ended in some dismal, distant region of London never charted by Baedeker and probably by no one else.

By taking matters in my own hand and hiring a hansom, in which I proudly rode for the first time, I fared better the next day. For the first time I viewed many of the buildings which were more familiar to me through reading than were the landmarks of New York, where I had already lived for two years. We were favored with a view of Queen Victoria riding in Rotten Row,

Hyde Park; and later, in Regent Street, we saw the Prince of Wales on a shopping tour.

We saw, too, considerable drunkenness in the streets, besotted men and women reeling along. It was a surprise to me that alcoholism was allowed to rage so freely. The conditions which permitted young women to serve intoxicants at the bar were so alien to my anticipations that I was sickened. It seemed to me that Queen Victoria, whom we in America regarded as one of the best types of womanhood and a powerful moral influence, was remiss in not condemning such conditions.

The residential district of San Francisco has no saloons, all of them being concentrated on the Barbary Coast. When I came to New York the extent of drunkenness there had shocked me. London, however, convinced me that drunkenness was not exclusively a characteristic of New York; on the contrary, that it was mild in degree as compared with its prevalence in London.

In London we met many of Dr. Kohut's old friends: Chief Rabbi Adler, Moses Gaster, Dr. S. Singer, Asher Myers, editor of the *London Jewish Chronicle* and self-appointed host to all visitors, Joseph Jacobs, Israel Zangwill, Professor Max Müller, famous Orientalist and author of a delightful book of memoirs which accompanies me wherever I go, and Professor Neubauer of Oxford, who had been helpful to my husband on his earlier visit.

Dr. Neubauer was an odd character. He had

insisted upon giving Alexander Kohut four shillings for his train fare to Ramsgate, then, in later years, scolded him roundly for not putting sufficient postage stamps on his letters. When we met him, we jokingly offered to reimburse him, and he actually accepted in a quite serious, matter-of-fact way.

After London, Paris, the city that has become a symbol for yearnings; a name that never loses its charm. Twenty-two subsequent visits to Paris had not dimmed the glamour of it for me.

But Paris, too, was remembered by my husband for an unsuccessful visit in the cause of his *Aruch*. The chief rabbi and numerous scholars had greeted him with warmth. Those, however, who might have been of material assistance had said bluntly: "We are not interested in Jewish science."

Our first hours in Paris, as in London, were given up to the all-absorbing *Aruch*, more proofs of which had to be read. Then we met Chief Rabbi Zadoc Kahn and visited Professor Joseph Derenbourg, whom I remember as a little man with snow-white hair and beautiful eyes that were sightless.

As it was a Friday, we attended Sabbath eve services at the chief rabbi's congregation in the Rue de la Victoire. In the seat next to me was Mme. Rothschild. After the services we were invited to the chief rabbi's home for dinner. My unfamiliarity with French made it necessary for my husband to translate the conversation. When they switched to German out of consideration for me, I was at least able to be an intelligent auditor. The chief rabbi and his family were very kind. During the conversation, he mentioned an interesting ceremony at which he had officiated some time before: that of the daughter of Ludovic Halévy, author of *"l'Abbé Constantin* and *Frou-Frou* and the son of Georges Bizet, composer of *Carmen.*

We had been in Paris only one day when the French press published as telegraphic correspondence from Vienna the news that the specialist we had meant to consult was dead. He had been stricken in a coupé while making a professional call. This news came as a blow, but my husband was much more resigned than myself. He assured me there were other physicians in Vienna just as capable, and his European trip would not be in vain. So far he had not suffered; the trip had given him new life; contacts with European scholars buoyed him up; the *Aruch's* progress was stimulating.

Vienna's call—which meant the call of Fanto's printing shop—was too strong to permit him to enjoy a stay of any length in Paris. So, without having done more than visit the Louvre several times and make a hurried trip to Fontainebleau, it was "on to Vienna."

In Vienna I began to feel that he knew altogether too many rabbis and scholars. He was a little too popular with them to suit me. I was left to roam about Vienna alone, while he spent his time with his fellow-Talmudists and in the shop of Fanto, printer of the *Aruch*. He wanted me to stay with him and his colleagues, but their learning was too obstruse for me. Or perhaps there were so many different brands of learning, and that was bewildering. It was like trying to tell the time by looking into a clock dealer's window where two hundred clocks, each set for a different hour, are on display.

Two of our visitors were Chief Rabbi Güdemann and Dr. Jellinek. The latter enjoyed the reputation of being the greatest expounder of homiletics in Europe. To this day his sermons are looked to as models of eloquence and style. In conversation I discovered that his wife was my father's first cousin. Through him I learned of other relatives, near and distant, notably Caroline Gumpertz-Tellheim, famous Viennese prima donna, who had retired to a castle in the suburbs, and only emerged in public once a year for a great concert at the Emperor's command, the receipts of which went to the poor. Dr. Jellinek arranged for me to visit her. It was like visiting royalty, the castle was so grand and the extensive grounds so lovely. A rare setting indeed for me to be in, and a romantic experience to meet this grande dame who herself showed me over the place, and displayed all her treasures, and told me stories of her life as a prima donna.

Unfortunately, we had lost the address of my father's younger brother, a physician living in a suburb of Vienna. But as I looked out of the hotel window the morning after our arrival in Vienna, my eye was caught by a tradesman's sign: Philipp Bettelheim. He proved to be a member of the Presburg branch of the family, and was able to give me my uncle's address. Soon I was among relatives, uncles, aunts, cousins, and I observed a striking resemblance between my father's sisters and myself. Two of their sons, as well as the son of my father's brother, were carrying out the family tradition in being physicians. Family pride and family affection having been a mark of ours from earliest years, I revelled in these associations. To one who had been so much informed concerning her ancestry and existing blood ties, and who had very few relatives in the United States, this communion was truly thrilling.

I had seen my people, and now I was to visit my husband's people. In the little village of Kecskemét in Hungary lived Alexander Kohut's mother, a woman of seventy-eight, whom he loved with all the capacity of his intense and expansive soul. One of the Ten Commandments is that children must love and honor their parents. But there is no commandment that parents must love their children; such a commandment is unnecessary. Alexander Kohut had such love for his parents as only parents have for children. He made repeated journeys to Kecskemét to receive his mother's blessing, regardless of distance or pressure of work and he derived great joy from his correspondence with her. He would lock himself in his room and weep for hours before the picture of his deceased father. And wherever he went, he carried his father's tobacco box with him, and earth from his father's grave.

It was in Kecskemét that this boy, so beautiful in his infancy that he was kidnapped by gypsies, received his first impetus towards scholarship. As the son, grandson, and grandnephew of Hebrew scholars, he had tradition behind him; and as the son of a man and woman of high character and extreme devotion, he had guidance and stimulus. From the father he inherited the powerful physique that from his early youth enabled him to toil so prodigiously. "*Vom Vater hab' ich die Statur, des Lebens ernstes Führen. . . .*" The son who could apply himself with such concentration to his task was the child of the man who, at the age of seventy, walked from Kecskemét to Vienna to speak to the King whom he had served for many years.

The train made innumerable stops at farmhouses, between great fields of wheat and vineyards where the grapes were grown that made the famous Tokay wine. Through the windows we could see the women working in the fields, wearing vivid red or blue calico skirts, short and full, and bandanna kerchiefs on their heads. Less frequently we glimpsed the men; lordly, gypsy-like fellows in sheepskin coats and full-pleated skirts.

As we approached our destination this son of Kecskemét was in a high state of excitement. It was good to watch his boyish eagerness, to see his brown eyes gleaming with joy and the color mantling his cheeks. I loved the naïve manner in which he asked me if he looked well. Of course he did! If he had been in the most wretched of spirits, he would nevertheless have called upon his will and his physical resources to bring life and animation to his face, for the sake of the moment of meeting with his mother.

The entire village seemed to have come to the station to meet the train. When my husband looked at the upturned faces he forgot my existence completely and jumped out of the coupé with a joyous shout, leaving me to follow with the aid of the conductor. I felt of little importance here beside this man who was meeting his own, but I was happy to stand silently by and watch them rejoice in each other's presence. I was eager to meet his mother and sister, though at the same time I dreaded it, for they spoke no English or German and I no Hungarian. However, his mother was very much absorbed in her son. I saw the great big man sitting in her lap as though he were a child, and recounting his many experiences in the United States, omitting the sorrows and struggles. It was in all earnestness that she said she would never forgive Columbus for having discovered America—America which took her son away from her.

We sat in the garden, which was in the courtyard of the little house. The picture of Alexander Kohut giving an account of his travels, of the neighbors looking out of windows into the courtyard and loitering at the gate, of the table loaded with delicacies that the dear little woman remembered he had loved as a small boy, moves me whenever I recall it.

That afternoon we were taken on a tour of the village of low, red-roofed houses. Kecskemét, as I recall it from this and subsequent visits, had two main characteristics, one of which reminded me of New York. Its streets were always being dug up and repaired, or just merely dug up. The other characteristic of Kecskemét was that there was always an army of geese marching up and down the main street. This, I hasten to add, suggests no comparisons.

The geese, I learned, were just as much a hometown product in Kecskemét as furniture is in Grand Rapids and health in Battle Creek. I was informed that the principal export of the village was goose livers for *pâte dé foie gras;* that, in fact, the village was really the goose-liver center of the universe, supplying Paris, Budapest, Vienna and other large cities. Being an American, I immediately began to think up schemes for developing a goose with ten or twelve livers. It hurt my American sense of efficiency to see so large a proportion of goose to liver, and I felt that under the existing conditions the problem of what to do with the rest of the fowl must have been grave enough to keep the population awake nights. They solved the problem, of course, by eating it. Throughout the village goose was the principal article of diet three times a day.

My husband's mother was aggrieved when she learned that in New York we used beef fat for frying. She led me aside and whispered that there was no fat like goose fat, and if I wanted Alexander Kohut to thrive, I must not fail to use it.

As we walked through the village in the evening, the air was filled with music. From every home came the sound of the violin, the 'cello, or the xylophone. We heard the Hungarian national hymn and the gypsy songs that Liszt immortalized and made international. The weird *csárdás* to which the men and women danced reached our ears, and our own pulses beat with the fury of that music which caused men and women to whirl until exhaustion overtook them.

In Kecskemét, as everywhere in Hungary, the lot of the women was infinitely harder than that of the men. The male seemed to have an easy time of it. Here I had my first view of a woman and a dog hitched to a cart, drawing supplies. Not far away from where we were stopping, women were building a house, the only men upon the premises being the supervisors.

That was thirty-six years ago. The women are still slaves there. Last year, when I visited Hungary on a pilgrimage to the graves of Alexander Kohut's parents, the picture had not changed. True, the people have doffed the picturesque garb of ancient Hungary and adopted the conventional costume of Europe, but social institutions remain about the same. It would have been preferable had they kept their old costumes and changed their mode of thought. But the night still resounds with the music that inspired Liszt, and while that remains, Hungary will be Hungary. And the geese still monopolize the main highway.

I have jumped thirty-six years forward, and must leap as suddenly back, finding myself still in Kecskemét. We enjoyed tremendously our stay in the little house, which was just as my husband had left it. On the top shelf of the cupboard were a few of the volumes of the Ersch and Gruber Encyclopedia, always reminding the mother of the two youngsters, Alexander and Adolph, who had left the family hearth to throw down the gauntlet to the material world. She felt aggrieved when anyone took a volume from its accustomed shelf. The Ersch and Gruber Encyclopedia remained in its accustomed place until the family home was deserted some twenty years later.

In the little town was the blind Hebrew teacher, Reb Loew, who had given young Alexander Kohut his first lesson. The rising scholar and rabbi never forgot his old teacher, and until the end of his life sent him a gold coin once a year. It was a happy meeting between the old and the young man.

Another of Dr. Kohut's friends was the Bishop of Kecskemét, who came to the synagogue of the town to hear my husband deliver a sermon the day after his arrival. The synagogue was jammed, people coming from miles around to listen to the words of Kecskemét's great son, who had returned to his people.

Poignant and tearful our good-byes. It was heart-breaking to look at the little woman to whom her son meant so much, and to think that for only a few days could she rejoice in his being near her.

Our destination was Carlsbad, where we stayed four weeks while my husband took the cure. In Carlsbad we were met by my brother Felix, who had left Panama some months earlier to take up special studies in the schools of Berlin and Vienna. His progress during his years at Panama had been remarkable, and he looked forward, when his European year should be over, to taking up the practice of one of the most noted California surgeons. It was wonderful to be with my favorite brother again. The Carlsbad stay is altogether memorable for its happiness. My husband had the comradeship there of his old teachers and friends, the historian Graetz, the scholars Kaufmann, Brann, Bacher, and Goldziher. He revelled in their company. Another who was much in our company was Gustav Karpeles, the young and rising Jewish historian, who told me much about Jewish literature.

In this my first trip abroad, I did not see very much of Europe as a tourist does; but its memories are dearer to me than that of the sum total of all the subsequent trips, in which I saw much more. As I look back upon it, despite its hurry and momentary vexations, it all seems touched with an ineffable charm.

Chapter x

LUCK'S PERSECUTIONS

I BELIEVE I returned from Europe better equipped to resume my life at 39 Beekman Place. The vacation had given me perspective. I could sit back, as it were, and reflect on what I had been doing. Enabled for the while to look back upon that intense year in a somewhat detached spirit, to see it as a whole and determine where my zeal was apt and where misapplied, I could bring more knowledge to my future work.

As a spiritual helpmate, too, I had improved. Before the trip, I had known the husband and father, the preacher in the pulpit, the scholar in his study. Now I had seen the man in the atmosphere of his past career, as son, as spiritual leader, as friend.

Despite all the cares of the household, the supplying of the wants of ten persons, supervision of the family sewing, entertaining of my husband's guests, and the visits of my family, I managed to find time to help him carry forward his influence. To lessen his burden and increase his opportunity for work upon the *Aruch*, I assumed charge of his extensive correspondence. There was so much demand for him as a public speaker that if he had acceded to all requests he would not have had a minute for even his congregational duties. It was my part to "decline with regrets."

About this time President Seth Low of Columbia University and my husband became good friends. President Low seriously discussed with him the possibility of his accepting a lectureship at the university. My husband, though grateful for the offer, was obliged to decline. In later years I derived considerable pleasure and satisfaction in taking an active part in the campaign which elected Seth Low Mayor of New York.

Newspapers sought interviews with Dr. Kohut upon various subjects and were eager to publish his Sabbath sermons. They were still being delivered in German, and I undertook to translate them. He was mastering the language of the country rapidly, but could not venture to preach in English until he could somewhat approach the excellence of his style in the more familiar tongue. No easy task had I selected. Hardly more than a novice at German, could I hope to reproduce in English, could I do justice to, that brilliant, seemingly effortless style? I commenced my work without appraising the difficulties. My early efforts had to be rewritten four or five times before they approached the originals. My ideal was to achieve the translation with only two rewritings.

His sermons were always interesting. He hated

alike obscurity of expression and ponderous rhetoric. For the thousands who thronged his temple, the knowledge of the centuries was humanized and made significant. He shook the dust from the past. So deep a student of history could not but illumine his subject. A series of his discourses known as *The Ethics of the Fathers* has, happily, been preserved within book covers. Read today, they awaken no less a response than when they were delivered before large and intent audiences three and four decades ago. If the words of most preachers are ephemeral, these particular words seem to apply as well today as when they were uttered.

I must state that by the time I became proficient as a translator of German, my services were no longer required. Dr. Kohut's progress was rapid. He knew that the younger members of the congregation preferred sermons in English, and it was not long before their pastor was able to satisfy the desire.

Every Sunday evening we attended services at Christian churches and listened to the sermons of well-known preachers. We heard all the eloquent clergymen of the day. This, more than anything else, accelerated my husband's use of English. And these Sunday evenings were a pleasure, too. We gained the friendship of some of the preachers, notably Dr. S. S. MacArthur of Calvary Baptist Church, Dr. DeWitt Talmage, Dr. Charles Eaton and Minot J. Savage, the gifted

Luck's Persecutions 157

and eloquent Unitarian. I think some of the devout members of our congregation might have charged us with heresy had they seen us at these services, particularly when our voices chimed in with those of the others during the singing.

That year we made the acquaintance of a young man whose personality created a remarkable impression upon my husband. A wealthy resident of Syracuse, New York, named Samson Simpson, left a considerable bequest in his will for a rabbinical college. A young Syracuse lawyer volunteered his services and offered to secure the bequest for the Jewish Theological Seminary. He came to New York to consult my husband on some rabbinical points of law necessary in the preparation of the case. It was a revelation to Dr. Kohut to meet this young man of brilliant promise who was willing to make such sacrifices without thought of fee or even reimbursement of expenditures. He predicted that Louis Marshall would become one of the greatest of Americans and one of the greatest of Jews. The truth of that prediction is to-day a matter of common knowledge. Mr. Marshall's extraordinary ability and his time, two factors for the possession of which many would be glad to pay a king's ransom, have always been at the command of the Jewish people in its hour of need. As one of the most distinguished members of the American bar his fame is nationwide. In the cause of Jewish relief and as a champion of the oppressed of Europe, he has given of himself unstintingly, without thought of glory. Glory is his, nevertheless.

Over our house there spread those first sad signs of the passing years, when the fledglings grow up and fly away to nests of their own. Gisela, the eldest daughter, as a result of a visit to members of my family in Richmond, was to marry the son of Moses Millhiser, president of my father's old congregation there. The young man was a school chum of my brother. It seemed as if fate had intertwined the destinies of the Kohuts and the Bettelheims. It was a little incomprehensible to Alexander Kohut, immersed in his work, that some of his children had suddenly grown up. He was delighted, however, with Gisela's happiness.

His health grew worse, and again we had recourse to a European trip and a stay at Carlsbad. Once more we spent sweet, tender days with his mother in the old home. The family group was completed by the presence of his only brother, Adolph. Two such opposites in one family I had never seen. Where Alexander Kohut was careful, Adolph was reckless. Not for him the prodigious toil of a quarter of a century over one task. He must have enjoyment today, though he pay the score in suffering tomorrow. His was the nature of a Heine. The most serious situations in life were things to take with apparent frivolity. He laughed at his failures and disappointments and they were many. Gifted with unusual abilities, he had a genius for getting into trouble, for kicking over the traces and making enemies at a time when he needed friends. He, too, was to be a rabbi. His temperament, however, was against him. A student at the Breslau Seminary, where his older brother had studied under Graetz and Frankel, he could not resist the temptation to enliven things. He wrote a satire about the teachers and the teachers' wives. It was a brilliant philippic, painful to the subjects. He was dismissed from the Seminary. Journalism became his profession. His ability commanded immediate attention, and his success was remarkable. He rose to the editorship of the *Berliner Zeitung* and enjoyed intimacy with Bismarck. But he would not suppress his satire. Just as he had scoffed at his teachers, he now scoffed at Bismarck. The barbs pierced the Iron Chancellor's skin, and he retaliated by ordering Adolph Kohut's expulsion from Germany. Later Bismarck permitted him to return, but the friendship was not resumed. He devoted himself to the writing of books, some of which were of real literary and historic value. He became a writing machine, turning out thousands of words a day for bread. He laughed, he snapped his fingers at life. His marriage to a Düsseldorf court singer, a Christian, saddened his brother considerably. The singer and the writer quarreled. "Elizabeth and I are celebrating our thirty years' war," Adolph once wrote Alexander Kohut. Hunger was no unusual experience for him; yet after weeks of privation he could take a sum of money which might maintain him for a month and spend it in a single night, with hunger staring him in the face thereafter. His wife was reduced to giving singing lessons, appearing before her pupils in the costumes of Marguerite, Ophelia and other rôles sung by her in opera. She was a shrew, but she loved him. Perhaps it was his laughter and seeming unconcern over adversity that incited her to battle. Undoubtedly picturesque in novels, it is a bit maddening when there is no food in the house, and no money.

We went to Carlsbad and while my husband was undergoing treatment we received a letter from the second daughter, Helen, asking our consent to her engagement to a splendid young man who was one of an interesting group visiting our home.

There were other important developments during the trip. A reputable and enterprising publishing firm, S. Calvary, of Berlin, made arrangements with Dr. Kohut for the sale and distribution of the *Aruch Completum*. I participated in the negotiations, and felt very proud when my husband stated that my presence had much to do with the successful outcome. The publishing firm also agreed to pay for the printing of the last volume. Thus a tremendous burden of financial worry was lifted, and we could breathe easier.

Luck's Persecutions 161

Not only was the *Aruch* the oldest child in that it received the greatest amount of attention, but it also caused the most concern. Despite the help of many interested individuals and the sale of the volume to a large number of scholars, the *Aruch* had drained the family's funds. Jewish publications did not pay, except in spiritual returns. Through the aid of Jacob H. Schiff, Dr. Gustav Gottheil, and Dr. Kohut's congregation, the printing of three volumes had been subsidized. Now that the last volume had been paid for and efficient distribution to scholars assured, we were in high spirits. There was still considerable work to do in manuscript, but the end was in sight.

We returned home happier for our material blessings, and therefore perhaps healthier. The tides of fortune had turned so much that Dr. Kohut said: "Luck is actually persecuting me." In addition to the news about the oldest daughter's engagement and the sale of the *Aruch*, we had also heard while abroad that our home had found a purchaser. Although charmingly located and full of romantic associations, the Beekman Place residence with its heavy mortgage represented too much of a financial burden. The news that it had been sold was welcome.

In October the wedding took place. Our daughter Gisela was a girl of rarest beauty, as tall as her father, with forget-me-not blue eyes and wavy hair of golden brown. She was but a few years younger than myself, and I was as proud of her as if she were my own daughter. There had been weeks of busy preparation. The ceremony was to be performed at the Temple, with my husband officiating, and all the rabbis of New York had been invited to attend.

That afternoon, just before Gisela changed to her wedding gown, we enacted a little ceremony among ourselves. The bride, her sisters and brothers and her father and myself assembled in the library. With a blessing and a few words from her father, we presented her with a beautiful Bible bound in white morocco. All of us made inscriptions, including the youngest child, whose hand had to be guided. Taking the pen I wrote with tired and trembling fingers: "May God bless you. I have done the best I could." I wrote it spontaneously, but I meant it. I wanted her to realize that despite my many limitations—of which I was conscious—I had meant well by her, and that out of a cup overflowing with love for her father, there was enough left for each of his children.

How wonderful she looked going down the aisle on the arm of her father, he in cap and gown, she in her bridal dress. Two persons so physically similar, yet in such vivid contrast. George and I followed. George gave the bride away.

Within a year Helen, too, was married.

Luck was persecuting him! On May 14, 1889, Alexander Kohut reached the great goal of his career. At 1 A. M. of that day the *Aruch* was completed in manuscript. Raising himself from his chair, where he had been working despite bodily pain, he offered up a fervent prayer. Then he called all of us up to his library. Each of us wrote one of the last remaining words, his hand guiding ours in the forming of the Hebrew characters. The last word was "bridge." He reserved this for his daughter, Valerie, who never forgot each night to bring refreshments to the scholar in his study.

"My dearest child, you were my bridge between life and death," he said. "Had you not looked after my wants, my light might long ago have been extinguished."

And thus was finished this stupendous work in eight volumes, containing four thousand double-columned pages, with an index and supplementary volume. His research had been conducted through the literatures of many nations, through ancient texts and medieval commentaries; it may be said that he had examined and studied almost every piece of literature dealing with Hebraism in all of a dozen languages.

This *Aruch*, which corrected many misleading errors in Hebrew literature and gave illuminating philological comment, was acclaimed "a monument of science" by Professor Friedrich Müller. Professor Franz Delitzsch declared it would only be appreciated at its full value a hundred years later. High praise was given it by scholars like

Buber, Brüll, Smolensky, Graetz, Ernest Renan, Barth, Kautzsch and Ascoli.

Boundless Alexander Kohut's happiness that the great task was finished; that task for which he had given his spirit, his body, his waking and sleeping hours.

Even the youngest member of the family felt a thrill of joy and relief. The children all saw that it meant their father's return to them, and they looked forward to happy days with no urgent duties in the library to stand between them.

There were even celebrations of a formal nature: the *Aruch* was attended ceremoniously. Congregation, family, friends joined in observing the event. The festivities lasted three days. The first day was entirely *en famille*. My parents and two sisters came from Baltimore to take part. We sang, romped, danced, got up an impromptu playlet, took part in the games of the children. It was Maytime in our hearts as well as on the calendar. Each of the children had prepared a present and a little speech for the father. The gifts ranged from carpet slippers to an easy-chair in which he could spend his newly won leisure. What joy welled up in us to see his life-dream realized, and to know that henceforth he would not labor under such continual strain.

The next day the event was celebrated by the congregation. Several other rabbis assisted in the service. My husband thanked the congregation for its patience with him, and said that the end-ing of the task would enable him to devote himself henceforth entirely to the duties of the Temple. The following day, Sunday, there was a gathering of friends at the house, and addresses were made by the Reverend Dr. Gottheil and Jacob H. Schiff, who had been so helpful in furthering the completion of the *Aruch*. Ofttimes as I look back upon the years that followed, as their trials and sorrows re-enact themselves before my mind's eye, I remember those three happy days, those days of spontaneity and expanding souls, and I feel that they compensated for everything.

Chapter xi

THE MEMORIAL LIGHT

THE time was approaching when we had to vacate our house. There are few moments in life more poignant than leaving a home which has many tender associations; especially the first home of a bride.

The oldest daughter had married; and the saddening shadows of family disintegration already hovered over the Beekman Place house. Though we saw our daughter frequently on her visits from Richmond and rejoiced over her happiness, yet something in the home seemed to have gone forever. Space and time seemed to be triumphing over the unity of flesh and blood.

We secured a house on Seventy-second Street. But what a wrench in parting! The last hour of the last day I went to my room and looked up and down the East River. It was autumn, a season overwhelming in its effect upon the sentiment of farewell. The picnic boats had deserted the river; gaiety was gone. Our little summer-house in the garden, decorated with leaves, hollyhocks, creepers, seemed particularly plaintive; for the moment it appeared to have a personality and a sad consciousness that it was being deserted. No longer would we sit there on quiet summer evenings and sip tea as we watched the lights of the passing boats.

My husband and the boys guarded the precious volumes of the library which taxed the capacity of two huge trucks. Two of the younger boys rode like sentinels atop them. When they returned from the new house, they found me in tears; I had been moved so by thought of leaving the old home and the river view. Yet I had been practical enough to insist that the house should be sold; I was sentimental enough to cry over it when the thing was done. You cannot sell your cake and have it; but you can weep. The little girl who was told "it's no use crying over spilt milk" must have felt that her natural and inalienable rights were being interfered with.

In February of 1890 my brother Felix returned from his year in Europe with the mark of death upon him. His life in the tropics, despite the beauty and robustness of his young manhood, had made deep inroads upon his health. The Isthmus of De Lesseps was not yet the sanitated locality of the Gorgas-Goethals triumphs. Disease lurked everywhere, slaying its thousands. As one of the principal physicians associated with the engineering project, my brother was ever on the fighting line against the common enemy. Now he, too, was stricken. He had contracted a tropical liver complaint and had hardly arrived in New York when he realized that he was perhaps hopelessly ill.

The days and nights of the next two weeks were devoted to nursing him. At his request, our parents were not informed of the seriousness of the situation. Our family physician, Dr. Isaac Adler, was called in. A hushed and saddened family awaited the findings of his visits. After several weeks of struggle, he advised to us to take my brother home to Baltimore. I accompanied him there.

How heart-rending his haggard appearance and dejection, in contrast with his beauty and animation a year before in Carlsbad, where he had talked joyously of the future awaiting him in San Francisco as assistant to one of California's great surgeons. We had had one little disagreement in Carlsbad which was now brought poignantly back to memory by him. During a conversation while sitting in Alte Wiese Park, I lamented the fact that our father had contributed no great memorial to scholarship, and that the world would perhaps never learn of his truly remarkable qualities. Felix was indignant. He disliked intensely my indulging in even a suggestion of a criticism of our father, and he begged me never to revert to the subject.

One year later, in New York, as we were being conveyed in a cab to the railway station, he remarked irrelevantly: "I think you were right in what you said about Father when we were in

Carlsbad. I was angry, but I reflected after you left. And why did Father give no monumental work to the world? Because of us. He made his love of scholarship subservient to his love for his children, and he gave to us the time and attention that might have made his name immortal among scholars. And if I recover, I'll see to it that father will be able to spend the rest of his days doing the things he wants to do."

It was a broken family in Baltimore that watched the patient struggle with death. The great William Osler came four times a week to attend him. He came not only because of scientific interest in the tropical disease which was gradually taking my brother's life, but because, as he so often said, "his life was well worth saving." Dr. Adler made several visits from New York, but all efforts failed. The disease did not respond to treatment or operation. In his delirium my brother kept repeating over and over again: "Is this 1428 McCulloh Street?" Upon being answered in the affirmative, he said: "I'm so glad to be home." After a long period of unconsciousness, he cried:"Blessed be the name of the Lord, for His mercy endureth forever."

On Passover eve, his twenty-ninth birthday, Felix Bettelheim, the beautiful, loving and beloved brother and son—the brilliant, kind young man with numberless friends—departed this life. We sanctify our dead if we love them; they become our saints and receive our worship for the rest of our lives. He lies next to our mother in the Richmond cemetery. Dr. Thorington, an eminent medical colleague, honored my brother's name by dedicating a text-book to his memory.

All Passover eves since his death have been for me an intermingling of the emotions of the sacred past. With the joy of the traditional festival is intertwined joy for the birth of this brother, gratitude for the memory of his nobleness, sorrow that he was cut off when he had no more than crossed the threshold of life.

When he died, I made the pledge to myself that I would endeavor to take my brother's place in the family, and by giving my father encouragement and financial aid carry out the son's wishes. I was determined to find the wherewithal to provide leisure for my father for scholarly research. How this was to be done, I did not know at the time.

Scholarship was the furthest thing from my father's mind. The son's death placed its mark upon him. He became suddenly old, and walked the streets in a preoccupied manner, failing to recognize people with whom he was wont to exchange cheery greetings. It was a tremendous effort, even, to go to the Temple on the Sabbath and meet the members of his congregation. And he had been so proud of his congregation. From the time he assumed the rabbinate there, it had grown steadily in attendance and spiritual value

The Memorial Light

until its place of worship became inadequate. A new site was secured at Madison Avenue and Robert Street, and a beautiful structure, modeled after the great synagogue in Budapest, was erected. But his vital interest was gone, and with depression, his health sank. I went to Baltimore as often as twice a week in an effort to cheer up my parents. It seemed to help but very little.

After much entreaty, Father was persuaded to make a trip to Europe to visit his brothers and sisters. Two Catholic priests, his friends, added their suasion to ours, and the three of them finally agreed to go together. They sailed from Baltimore.

Three days out a Russian Jew in the steerage died. Arrangements were made for a burial at sea. My father pleaded with the captain that the passenger's body be saved for his family, which was awaiting him at Bremen. "You wouldn't do this to a first-class passenger, or to one of the priests, or to myself, a rabbi. I fear it is because he was only a poor devil in the steerage." The captain assured him that the rule for burials at sea applied to all passengers.

This occurred in June, 1890. My father traveled on the Continent with the priests; then they separated, he going to Vienna to visit his relatives. In August they met once more and commenced the return journey. At Bremen they embarked aboard the steamship *Muenchen*, bound for Baltimore.

On August twenty-first my father died suddenly at sea, of Bright's disease. The priests pleaded with the captain that his body be saved for his family. But he was buried at sea in the American flag.

The priests, who had studied Hebrew with my father, read the Hebrew burial service over his body. They read it from his prayer book. As they opened the book, a small American flag dropped out.

It was an eager family that went to the pier to meet the expected father; a stricken family that learned he was no more.

A great memorial service was held in Baltimore, with my husband delivering an impassioned eulogy. As the *American Hebrew* reported:

> It appeared that all Baltimore, Jew and Christian, wished to do honor to his memory, for the building was crowded to its fullest possible capacity before the services began, and the doors had to be closed. Members from nearly all the Jewish choirs took part in the service, and the ministers, officers and members of nearly every congregation were in attendance, while many Christians also were present. The pulpit and Dr. Bettelheim's chair were appropriately draped.
> Reference to the death of Dr. Bettelheim was made on Sabbath last in New York and Philadelphia by nearly every minister.

The year of 1890 was given over to tears. My sisters and I planned to keep the memorial light burning for at least a year, and against my husband's protests and to his sorrow, I indulged in this morbid fancy.

The Memorial Light

To ease my pain, I engaged in public activities, threw myself into whatever offered forgetfulness. The Women's Health Protective Association had extended its field to cover the general health situation in New York. I joined them in their militant campaigns against inefficient street cleaning, accumulation of garbage cans, and other negligence dangerous to the public health.

Soon opportunity came to be useful in a service for which I had the necessary background and experience. Dr. Gustav Gottheil had the year before organized the Emanu-El Sisterhood. He invited me to attend several of the meetings. Realizing that an organization of this kind gave women opportunities for worthy service among the poor, I urged upon my husband that a similar group be formed among the women of his congregation. It seemed to be the work that I could do for him, and he consented. So there was a meeting of the women of the congregation, and after an explanatory address by Dr. Gottheil, the second sisterhood of American Jewish women was organized, with myself as president. It is now called the Sisterhood of the Central Synagogue. This was the beginning for me of many years of service in Jewish activities.

The work was satisfying, for many reasons. It was an outlet for emotion over the loss of my brother and father, and I felt I was helping my husband, besides. It also brought back the days of the Fruit and Flower Mission in San Francisco when I entered the miserable hovels of the poor and felt joy in bringing them some relief.

The women associated with me responded to their new obligations enthusiastically. To many it was an entirely new experience. Charity had meant to them the indiscriminate doling out of money. But here, in the modest little Second Avenue flat, which served as a centre for the gathering-in of clothing and the administration of relief, we could feel that our giving was to some constructive purpose.

A small day-nursery and a kindergarten were established. Dr. Gottheil and the members of the Emanu-El Sisterhood offered splendid co-operation. We met often in conference, and by exchange of experience were able to achieve considerable progress in our methods. Sisterhoods were organized in other congregations and all through the United States. A unified program was a natural development. In New York co-operation with the United Hebrew Charities followed. For a more efficient service, the city was districted, and to our Sisterhood was allotted the zone from Houston to Fourth Streets.

The President of the United Hebrew Charities was that fine gentleman who lived to a ripe old age, Henry Rice. Many noted members of the Jewish Community were included in its directorate. Isaac Isaacs, whose father, Rev. M. S. Isaacs, founded the *Jewish Messenger*, was secretary.

Whenever I felt I could be spared from home duties, I went down to the sisterhood headquarters, in what was then to us a pretentious house on Third Street near First Avenue. We were neighbors of other organizations, such as the House on Henry Street, the centre of the great nursing service internationally known as the work of Lillian D. Wald, the Hebrew Free School, Minnie D. Louis Downtown Sabbath School, which later became the Hebrew Technical School for Girls, and a number of other religious schools, which had been established hurriedly to meet the needs of the children of immigrants.

There was fascination in walking along Hester, Canal, Grand, Allen, Varick and Essex Streets and East Broadway, and losing one's self in the throngs of newcomers to America. The persecutions in Russia and Roumania had caused the exodus of thousands. They peopled the narrow streets and squalid tenements which had been the abode of earlier immigrants, chiefly Irish and Germans, immigrants who had also known oppression. English landlordism and the Corn Laws had sent a wave of Irish migration westward. The failure of the Revolution of 1848 in Germany had given liberals the choice of either remaining there and suffering from the vindictiveness of the restored tyranny, or seeking their future in a more benign environment. Among the German immigrants of this wave was a man who became one of America's greatest statesmen

—visit the noble statue and memorial to him in Morningside Park, New York—Carl Schurz.

Each of these early waves of immigration had been met with opposition in certain American quarters. Those who had been here a little longer set up a cry as early as 1820 that the country was being overrun with foreigners, and that they were so inferior to the native stock that the country would suffer. The same sort of scepticism that has been expressed in recent years about Eastern and Southern Europeans was expressed in those early years about the immigrants of that period. Fear is the commonest of human failings, and its most common manifestation is a dread of the unlike. Those arrivals in the early history of the republic soon proved their worth. Later waves of immigration to the land of tolerance have also contributed richly to our nation's life.

To the East Side, then, to the traditional abode of each successive group of immigrants, came these Jews from Russia and Rumania. I had an intense interest in them from the first week I was in New York, when I visited the great receiving station at Castle Garden with Emma Lazarus and Reverend Dr. H. Pereira Mendes.

I had of course heard a great deal about Emma Lazarus and also knew her writings, especially from the *Jewish Messenger* and the *American Hebrew*, which printed everything she wrote and gave long accounts of her visits to Castle Garden with Michael Heilprin. After my arrival in New

York I visited her home with Dr. H. Pereira Mendes, and, to my surprise, found that there were five daughters and one son. Sarah Lazarus, though she did not make for herself any great reputation except in her immediate circle, was also a remarkable woman. And there was Josephine, the younger sister, who continued Emma's literary traditions by making frequent contributions to the magazines of remarkable essays on Jewish questions. She wrote several papers for the Council of Jewish Women and appeared regularly at the meetings during the first years of the Council's activities.

As for Emma Lazarus, I found her so reserved and timid that she almost gave the impression of being actually afraid. I often wondered since whether she was not afraid, afraid because of the persecutions that had driven her people to huddle like forlorn animals in the foul and dark tenements of New York. As a matter of fact, it was these persecutions that had aroused her race consciousness and made her the supreme poetess of Jewish suffering. When she awoke to her Jewishness, she took lessons in Hebrew from Sarah Lyons, who found her so apt a pupil that she engaged Professor Ehrlich for her as her teacher. With his help she became a proficient student of the Bible in the Hebrew language.

I believed I could even recognize among the people who visited the Sisterhood house some of the very individuals I had seen coming down the gangway of the ships at the Battery. Life in the New World had been very unkind to some of these arrivals. Many who had been rabbis and scholars in Europe experienced the greatest difficulty in fitting themselves into the economic pattern. It was a bitter struggle. As was natural, these families of rabbis and students were of particular interest to me.

I carried a sense of the practical along with my idealism and emotionalism, and I am willing to confess that I induced many an erudite scholar to join the army of sweatshop laborers in preference to being reduced to destitution.

Many who had been misled by glowing accounts of America were grievously disappointed. At home they had known no such misery, no such squalor. Moreover, they missed the religious life which had been so great a part of their European background. Often, in making my rounds as an investigator for the Sisterhood, I stumbled into the little makeshift synagogues, and came upon groups of old men and women who were beyond the age of adaptation to conditions, and who mourned the passing of the old order in their lives. I asked them: "Why do you sit in synagogues all day long?" Their answer was: "We hoped to find the Promised Land in America. We must continue to pray, and turn our faces once more toward the East."

To me, as I recalled the San Francisco past, it seemed that the wretched hovels of Barbary Coast were by far preferable to the tenements of the East Side, whose creaking stairs we climbed flight after flight, and whose spaces were divided and subdivided into tiny cubicles called rooms, without air or daylight.

Dr. Kohut, who was more in demand as a speaker than ever, was invited to dedicate a synagogue in Boston. The congregation was to be housed in a church previously presided over by Edward Everett Hale, author of the famous story, *The Man Without a Country*. I was eager to go, not only because it meant a visit to New England but also because of the opportunity to meet the man whose story had been such a favorite of ours, particularly my father's. He and I had had many discussions over the fate of Philip Nolan, and had disagreed over his punishment, I saying it was too harsh, Father holding emphatically the opposite. He felt that no crime could be greater than lack of love of one's country.

The visit was a great pleasure to us. We viewed all the historic spots—Faneuil Hall, Bunker Hill—visited Harvard University and stood under Washington's elm tree. Then the visit to the home of Henry Wadsworth Longfellow, and reception by "Alice with Golden Hair," one of the daughters in *The Children's Hour*. Her hair was silver, it is true, but at that particular moment it seemed to turn gold.

The meeting had been arranged by Dr. Hale. As I stood in the poet's room, my thoughts leaped back to San Francisco and to Miss Hunt, who had given me a copy of *Outre Mer*, and I found myself repeating, as I have over and over again since then:

> Look not mournfully into the past;
> It comes not back again.
> Wisely improve the present, it is thine.
> Go forth into the shadowy future with a
> Manly heart and without fear.

We also visited the homes of Hawthorne and Emerson, and we saw the House of the Seven Gables, of which I had first learned from Miss Hunt.

Soon after the New England visit both of us received a "call" to another part of America—Chicago, where the World's Fair was to be held. The committee in charge of the Congress of Religions, for which a special building had been erected, invited my husband to deliver an address at the Congress and also asked for the volumes of the *Aruch Completum* to put into the permanent exhibit.

As for me, I was invited to read a paper at another congress at the Fair, the one invoked by the Jewish Women of America. The whole thing was thrilling—the idea of going to the great exposition and seeing so many wonders, and the honor done me in being asked to speak before co-religionists of my sex from all over the country.

The Memorial Light

I remembered my early doubts and my return to religion. My father, with his infinite patience and fervor, had awakened my religious consciousness, but it was my marriage to Alexander Kohut that had aroused in me a pride and glory in the faith of my people.

I gave considerable thought to the subject of my paper and put all my efforts into its preparation. Our plans, however, were upset. The doctor decided that my husband was not well enough to go; my sister, instead, should accompany me, and she and I were to leave for Chicago at midnight. At the dinner table Dr. Kohut looked unusually pale, and as the meal progressed seemed less and less able to bear up. Finally he said, almost with tears in his voice: "How shall we manage without you for a whole week?"

My heart gripped me at his absolute dependence, and his sadness. "I didn't really intend to go," I cried, impulsively. "Isn't it nonsense to travel twenty-four hours in order to read a fifteen-minute paper?"

He always took me literally, never questioning anything I said to him. It was his blind faith, his absolute certainty that whatever I told him was true, that always made me try to live up to the high standards he set for me.

"Why then," he said happily, but in a quiet tone, "did you allow me to be unhappy all day?"

An hour later my sister left for Chicago without me. She was to read my paper before the congress. I went to my room and wept. The disappointment was keen. Afterward, when I heard about the gathering of Jewish women, and of the splendid material for social service brought together by Hannah Solomon and Sadie American, and the welcome to Chicago by Emil G. Hirsch, I was sorrier than ever that I had not been present. But in later years I felt it was one of the finest sacrifices I had ever made for Alexander Kohut.

Chapter xii

BEYOND

THE next years were given over to the sick room. My husband's health grew steadily worse. His physician finally confided to George and me that he was suffering from cancer. Stricken at heart, we pledged ourselves to secrecy. We were the only two to be told. Our common secret and our solicitude for him made the boy my constant companion. His father's love for him, and his love for his father, and now my love for both of them, drew the three of us into an all-absorbing trinity of affection. My husband called his son his shadow, and was happy that he was studying with a view to following in his footsteps. Over and over again, Alexander Kohut, with a premonition of numbered days, begged me never to forsake the boy, who had always been the object of our greatest tenderness because of his delicate constitution. And when father and son were together, the older man made the youth promise that he would urge me to marry again and find a new happiness in life.

The sick room became a sacred place, and this

and the adjoining library, to which he tottered whenever his feeble strength permitted, were the only rooms in the house that existed for me. I lost interest in everything else, endeavoring only to ease his days. The Jewish women who had convened the congress during the World's Fair had invited me to join in forming the organization that was the outcome of the congress: the National Council of Jewish Women. But for fourteen months I never left my husband for an hour, and learned of the first tumultuous meetings of the women only from hearsay.

Illness, however, did not mean the cessation of his activity. He still received many callers: Jacob H. Schiff, Isaac M. Wise, Emil G. Hirsch, who was electrifying Chicago with his brilliant sermons; Judge Mayer Sulzberger, Elliott Shepherd, Sabato Morais, Gotthard Deutsch of Cincinnati, and many others. He continued his duties as professor of Talmud at the Jewish Theological Seminary, the students reporting to the sick room for instruction. Among them were Joseph H. Hertz, who has since become chief rabbi of England, and that incomparable leader and flaming spirit, Stephen S. Wise, now an international figure and the outstanding rabbi of America.

During these months, Dr. Kohut also wrote a great deal, notably two monographs, one of which was on the literature of the Yemenite Jews in Southern Arabia. The monograph attracted attention in the scholarly world long before Solomon

Beyond

Schechter, with his famous Genizah discoveries, and others, made the subject of Yemenite literature widely known.

Of all the friends who visited our home regularly there were two whose kindnesses he felt he could never repay. One was Jacob H. Schiff, who agreed so generously to print one of the volumes of the *Aruch;* the other was Gustav Gottheil.

Jacob H. Schiff was an extraordinary man. Though a world figure as a financier and a colossal factor in the industrial expansion and commercial ascendancy of America, he found time and energy for a vast amount of communal work. Other wealthy men have contributed magnificently to the upkeep of deserving institutions, but in addition to his financial bequests to Christian as well as Jewish causes and institutions, Jacob H. Schiff gave himself. He was careful to have an intimate knowledge of the workings of the various institutions in which he was interested, visited them frequently, and was ever watchful for their efficacy and progress. At his office he often gave as much time to a scholar or welfare worker as to a railway president. He respected all engagements and never gave his word idly, thinking it as important to be on time when he promised to meet a few school children as when he conferred with E. H. Harriman over the financing of the Union Pacific Railroad. But perhaps his greatest trait was his upstanding championship of the Jews the world over. When other Jews of his class were inclined to cringe before the Gentile world, he stepped boldly forward, and even used his influence to get the United States Government not to ratify a treaty with Czarist Russia because of its bloody persecutions of the Jews.

As for Dr. Gottheil's devotion to my husband, it is difficult to write adequately. That gracious, beloved personality whose congregation belonged to the Reform wing, was the first to extend a brotherly welcome to the man whom the adherents of Conservative Judaism had named their champion. His breadth of view and benevolence of spirit knew no measure. He and Alexander Kohut were "above the battle." It was he who called to Mr. Schiff's attention the value of my husband's writings, and he who sought to interest other friends in defraying the cost of the later volumes.

When my husband underwent an operation, Dr. Gottheil assured him that he and his colleagues would fill his pulpit until his recovery. For half a year he took on double duty—officiated at all synagogue functions, visited the members of my husband's congregation, performed all those services which a rabbi is called upon to make. After my many observations of the rather unbrotherly relationship between colleague and colleague not only in the ministry but in all walks of life, Dr. Gottheil was a heart-warming revelation.

That year might have been called one of spiritual preparation. The great sorrow that loomed over me somehow seemed to ease the pain arising from the passing of my brother and the tragic death of my father. The anguish was there, but in being able to serve there was temporary forgetfulness.

Then, too, I found what seemed to be almost happiness in having Alexander Kohut so much to myself. In earlier days preoccupation with the *Aruch* had put a distance between us. Now we lived for each other more than ever before. When his strength permitted, we would walk to Central Park, only a few blocks away, and spend wonderful hours sitting near the fragrant arbor of wistaria at West Seventy-second Street. It had been a life of ambition and tension, with little relaxation; now we rested and talked about it. In leisure, though enforced, Dr. Kohut could look back upon his crowded years and trace their pattern. To one whose life had been so rich in spiritual values, who had struggled manfully and suffered nobly, there was much to remember, a wide field for reflection. Though he had achieved greatly, he was humble, for he recognized the limitations of man, and admitted there was much in the human soul that was obscure and that he was powerless to understand. I felt he was overmodest and told him so. He revealed to me his innermost struggles on religious questions. He spoke frequently of the life of the hereafter and the immortality of the soul. Sometimes, in a spirit of naiveté, he promised to return in some way and let me know he was near.

As we walked slowly back after these hours that belonged to me, it seemed that in some unseen way my spirit had received new strength. In the early evening hours, as I sat at the window of his room and looked out upon the stars, I thought of the near future and wondered how I should manage. My duties seemed so light when he was there to give me courage, but without him . . . and then I felt that the doctors might be mistaken, and his life be spared for many years.

To keep occupied during the hours in the sick room, I reverted to early San Francisco pleasures, and began to paint wild flowers again. They were terrible daubs, but Dr. Kohut thought them wonderful, and assured me he forgot his pain while I was working.

Deciding that my painting was neither artistic nor useful, I sought some better way of applying the passing hours. It occurred to me that the study of English literature could serve more than a casual end. Lectures were "the rage," and some lecturers about whom their auditors "raved" were not so profound that they could not be equalled by persons of fair education and intelligence. I convinced myself that this might prove a desirable way of providing for the future. During these months I completed five lectures upon the Lake poets and five upon Victorian writers. They were crude and were prepared without adequate research, but I was comforted by the knowledge that they represented a possible avenue to an income. At any rate, they served an immediate purpose, and that was to divert the man in the sick room. I read them to him as well as other and decidedly better pieces of literature, among them nearly the whole of the monumental *History of the Jews* by Graetz, issued in English translation by the Jewish Publication Society of America.

He grew weaker and weaker, but would not leave off teaching the students of the Seminary. When informed the year before that he must submit to surgery, he requested that the operation be performed in his library, where he could look upon his bookshelves, filled with so many old, dear friends. And now that life was ebbing, he persisted in holding aloft the torch of scholarship. Up to the last moments of consciousness, Seminary students imbibed learning at his bedside. I recall the last lesson of Stephen Wise and George Kohut and Joseph H. Hertz a few days before Alexander Kohut's death. The teacher lay in bed, his hands too weak to hold a book. At the edge of the bed sat the young students, holding the heavy volume before Dr. Kohut's eyes. That year, which marked the end of Alexander Kohut's career, marked the beginning of Stephen Wise's. A few months before, when the anniversary of Rabbi Wise's thirtieth year of service was celebrated, my thoughts went back to that scene in the sick room, with the dying man passing on his torch of knowledge to the coming champion of Israel, who has ever cherished his teacher's memory.

His end was hastened by his insistence, one Sabbath, on leaving his sick room. The great Hungarian, Kossuth, had died. Alexander Kohut, who had been his friend, who had been called "the Jewish Kossuth," recalled the fevered days of Hungary's struggles for independence, and, though racked with pain, felt he must go to the Temple that Sabbath morning. He could not be kept away. He promised not to speak. The call, however, was too strong. At the end of the services he ascended the pulpit and delivered an impassioned address upon Kossuth and his relation to Judaism. When we saw how ardently he gave himself up to his subject, we were frightened. At the last words he collapsed, and had to be carried home. That was in March.

On May 25, 1894, a great soul passed from this world.

In accordance with his last wishes, the services were conducted by my father's schoolmate, the man who married my father to his second wife and who united Alexander Kohut and myself— Dr. Benjamin Szold. We were not alone in our grief.

The day after the funeral, George and I, contrary to the Jewish custom and oblivious of sacrilege, returned to the Linden Hill cemetery to visit our dead. I resented openly the visitations of the

Almighty upon me, unmindful of the loss that his eight children had sustained, and the loss to Judaism and the world. The pale, delicate boy tried to console me by reciting a verse:

> The living are the only dead.
> The dead live, nevermore to die,
> And often when we mourn them, fled,
> They never were so nigh.

I looked at him in amazement, realizing that *he* was prepared to comfort me and that *I* had no comfort to offer him. We walked slowly up the short hill to the grave. After reading the service, the boy took my hand, and in a voice which was stern, he said: "I am surprised and disappointed in you. You are selfish in your grief, and I know that our dear one never thought you could be selfish. You don't realize that we have lost our father. Your attitude of mind is not worthy of Alexander Kohut or of Rebekah Kohut. Try to be strong and do the things he would want you to do."

I looked at him, and the words of resentment which were forming died on my lips. "You are right," I said. "I'm going back and will begin all over again."

I did.

Chapter xiii

EMERGENCE OF THE JEWESS

IT WAS a summer of doubt and agony and loneliness. The men I had loved most, whose guidance had been a shining light in life, had been taken from the world. Brother, father, husband; all in four swift years. Though many friends came with sympathy and tried to lighten my sorrow, not only with words, but also with deeds, I felt alone, acutely alone.

"You have neither the means nor the right to indulge in grief." So said Dr. Isaac Adler, warning me not to let myself go under. "You were brave all through the trouble, and I admired you for it. Don't let me be disappointed in you now. You must find the lost threads, and pick them up as best you can, and remember: "I shall be your friend."

Though Dr. Adler had attended my husband every day for seven months, he refused to accept a fee. A man of few words, he gave most people the impression of being austere. I knew better. During those trying days in the sick room I discovered the real him. A soft glance, or the terse expression, "brave girl" or "good nurse," spoke

Emergence of the Jewess 193

volumes. In after years, when he, too, was battling against the chronic disease that took him off, I visited him frequently. He dropped the mask of austerity completely, and enjoyed recalling the Beekman Place days. It amused him to tell me how seriously I had taken myself and my work and he teased me for my unconsciousness of my shortcomings.

Whenever I was discouraged, or faced by a baffling problem, I would find an excuse to go to Dr. Adler. Great in medical knowledge, he was greater in his understanding of human psychology. He could size up a situation in a flash, and his advice was always worth following. When I assumed more worries than a person should, he laughed me out of my state of mind.

"Don't take yourself so tragically," he said once. "Do you want to go down in history as the best stepmother that ever lived? If you possessed three times your energy, and three times your ambition to devote yourself to your family, you'd still not secure the title. No one can."

That made me smile, of course, and I questioned whether there wasn't some truth in what he said—perhaps the smack of an overweening desire not to fail in anything I undertook. I had undertaken to be a stepmother; I *must* make the best of stepmothers.

But that wasn't all, was it? I asked myself. My father and husband had left me another heritage. In my loneliness I wrestled and groped.

Something must come, besides the sheer struggle with the economic situation, to fill the void. What could I do to carry on their work, to keep their spirit alive, to have them beside me always even if they were gone?

The answer to my queries did not come at that time. I saw no special fields in which I could do definite, concrete things in line with their humanitarianism and love of Jews and Judaism. I could not remotely dream that it was through the awakening of women that the spiritual solution should come, and that by the assertion of my Jewish womanhood as well as the Jewish womanhood the world over I should be carrying on the noble tradition handed down to me.

The immediate problem, however, was economic. The oldest son, George, was a mere lad whose health was such that he could only struggle to keep alive. The girls were helpless. We had some resources, but so limited that the day must be provided for when they would be exhausted. The six young children must not know want; the home, at all costs, must be kept intact.

Several months earlier, before leaving for Europe, Jacob H. Schiff had inquired about Dr. Kohut's condition and assured me he wished to be of service. After my husband's death I received a cable from him, then cruising off the coast of Norway, asking me to wait until his return before making definite plans for the future. This was encouraging, but my pride, amounting almost to vanity, made me try to do what I could, meanwhile, on my own account. I applied for various positions in city institutions, and even considered a journalistic career. After writing several articles for newspapers, however, I realized that the precarious existence of a freelance writer was not for me.

Then it struck me that the lectures I had written in my husband's sick room might be turned to good account. A fresh reading showed me that much recasting was necessary. So I spent days in the Columbia University Library at Forty-ninth street and Madison Avenue reading up more comprehensively on my subjects and revising the manuscript in accordance with more mature judgment.

The writing finished, the next thing was to secure the patronage of a well-known woman who would permit me to deliver the lectures in her home before an invited audience. Parlor lectures were the vogue, and in the home of the rich there were frequent gatherings of friends to listen to the addresses of various authorities and pseudo-authorities on divers subjects. There was no doubt that under the right auspices I could derive an income which would go part of the way toward providing our livelihood. Deep in my heart, I felt the amateurishness of my efforts, but it was no time to question one's abilities too closely. And in my trunk at home, to give me self-assurance, was a diploma from the Normal school of

San Francisco which mentioned my qualifications for teaching English literature.

The summer moved along slowly. Most of the people I knew were away, and I spent long days in planning for the coming months. The natural state of society is indifference; it is only through a concerted attack that we less favored ones can command its attention. The fate of the children and myself depended upon me, and I felt my responsibility and marshalled my forces accordingly.

I speak as though I were alone in a hostile world, friendless and ignored. Such was far from the case. I had friends, well-wishers, sympathizers, yet, in the last analysis, I was alone. My future depended upon myself. Great is humanity's capacity for self-absorption; not so great its capacity for genuine concern about others. Most human beings are kind; they will go half way to meet a person; but if that person is a shrinking individual who expects to be sought out in his retreat, he will learn a very tragic lesson in superfluity.

My dear friend Dr. Gottheil returned to New York and soon visited me. Here was an eager listener to my plans. He approved whole-heartedly and left promising to help. But over and above everything, I awaited with impatience the return of Mr. Schiff. I expected that he would visit us on the Jewish New Year, as he had always done. He did not disappoint me. He called on New Year's afternoon. I did not know

Mr. Schiff really well. It was my husband's friend that he had been, drawn to him by respect for his scholarship and personality. I wondered whether he would possibly transfer his friendship to me.

That New Year's afternoon I lost no time in telling him how necessary it was for me to earn money, how I had hunted for work, and that my efforts to write for newspapers had been unsuccessful. He listened without comment. Then I decided it was time to be bold, for the sake of my children. I mentioned the lectures I had prepared and asked whether I could not deliver them in his home under his wife's patronage.

To my dismay, he discouraged me. Another hope gone. The field of opportunities was gradually narrowing. I wondered which of my plans would materialize. Clearly, it was to be a hard struggle for existence. And just as clearly, so it seemed at the time, Mr. Schiff had no interest in the Kohut family, but had merely called to pay a formal visit of condolence to Alexander Kohut's widow.

How delightfully surprising, therefore, when two or three days later a note came from Mrs. Schiff saying she was deeply interested in my plan and would be pleased to have my lectures held in her drawing-room. The skies brightened.

The lectures were not to commence for several months. My oldest sister in San Francisco had been writing me letter after letter importuning me to pay her a visit. I had been unwilling to leave New York while there was uncertainty as to my future, but now that the lectures under favorable auspices had been arranged for, I was glad to go back to my old home. The strain of the previous year had told upon my health, and I felt that from my sister, who had always been like a second mother to me, I would gather new courage for the ordeal of life.

Eight years had passed since I had left San Francisco, fresh from the academic world. A girl of dreams, I had been put to no ordinary test in those years. The woman who returned had lived on an abnormal scale. She had risked all upon a great love and had known joys and heavy responsibilities and heavier sorrows.

I renewed my San Francisco friendships and found that here, too, life had marched on. Some it had seared, some crowned with glory. Others were as I had left them, merely older.

With Esther, sister of understanding spirit, I found peace. Whatever my experience of the last years, I was still the little sister to her, and she knew how to comfort and gladden little sisters.

And while I rested in the West, forces were at work in the East which were to bring the answer to my spiritual problems and put into my hands the means whereby I should always walk in the paths blazed by my father and husband and feel that they were constantly there with me, my deeply loved companions and leaders.

Emergence of the Jewess 199

As I have already said, a new factor had come into the life of Jewish women in America, the National Council of Jewish women. Each of the women who had taken part in the original World's Fair Congress had been charged with the organization of a Council section in her locality. While my husband was still alive, Minnie D. Louis had called an organization meeting in New York and had invited me to attend it. But at that time, I had no interest outside of my husband's sick room. I was later told of the clash that had occurred at the meeting, of the dissension between women of Orthodox and Reform beliefs, and the gloom over the differences, which seemed to preclude the successful organization of a New York section.

A few days after I arrived in San Francisco a telegram came from Minnie D. Louis asking me to accept the presidency of the New York section. I was not at the house when it arrived and my sister told me nothing of it as she wanted me to have a complete rest during my stay and not be concerned about the future. But she was proud and elated over the honor done me, and believed that the responsibility would give me the desired interest outside the home. So she wired back acceptance. A few days later there was another telegram from Mrs. Louis instructing me to stop at Chicago on the way East and confer with Hannah Solomon, the national president, and

Sadie American, the national secretary. This telegram, too, was withheld from me.

It was not until the end of my stay, when I was filled with new courage and the desire to live not in retrospect but in the problems of the present, that my sister broke the news. Conceive of my surprise. The thing was farthest from my thoughts. However, I approved of what my sister had done, and looked forward eagerly to my duties in this new movement which so completely had my sympathy. In Chicago I was apprised of everything that had developed since the National Council had been formed. The day after my arrival in New York the first meeting of the executive committee of the New York section was held. Mrs. Louis introduced me to the committee, most of whom were unknown to me, as I to them. Before the session was over, it was evident that we were all ardent Jewesses, anxious to make our contribution to the welfare of our people and the preservation of our religion.

It was a gathering of real Jewish women notables, women who, though they made a name for themselves in the world, were all lovable persons whom I think of with affection and tenderness.

There was Julia Richman, the brilliant educator whose name has been immortalized through the naming of a girls' high school in New York after her.

There was Minnie D. Louis, sweet singer in

Israel and Southern aristocrat, who, as I have already mentioned, founded the Hebrew Technical School for Girls.

There was Esther S. Ruskay, the fine poetess and fearless champion of Orthodoxy. Her home was always the stimulating centre of a young intellectual group.

There was Mrs. Frederick Nathan, later president of the Consumers' League, and Sarah Lyons and Minnie Isaacs, all three representatives of the Sephardic (Spanish-Portuguese) Jews, some of whom settled in America in pre-Colonial days and took part in the Revolutionary War. The father of Sarah Lyons was the minister of the Sephardic synagogue and was the childhood friend and neighbor of Emma and Josephine Lazarus. Minnie Isaacs, who became secretary of the council, and did her work with modest, quiet charm, was the daughter of Judge Myer S. Isaacs, whose father founded the *Jewish Messenger*.

Then there were two women who were among the first confirmants at Temple Emanu-El, Dinah Gitterman and the wife of Judge David L. Leventritt.

And finally there was one whom life brought closest to me of all and made my lifelong friend, though we had had a sharp clash of opinions the first time we met, and have had again several times since. That's the sort of person Hannah B. Einstein is. She has a marked individuality. There are no half-ways with her. Beautiful, radiant, maintaining a lavish house and table, you'd have taken her at first sight for a spoiled darling. The fact is that though she was born and raised in luxury, the sufferings of the poor, sufferings of any sort, obsessed her. I truly believe that the reason she was first drawn to me was that I wore a widow's veil.

She and I had come together at the Emanu-El Sisterhood, where she was for giving without too many questions asked. But the world had outgrown indiscriminate alms-giving; the era of "scientific charity" had begun, in which the head must rule—but not stifle—the heart. If a poor girl wanted a silk dress with a train, Mrs. Einstein was for giving her the silk dress and the train. My idea was to help the girl to secure the silk dress and the train herself by her own efforts. (Though, as a rule, when people work for a thing, they outgrow, metaphorically speaking, silk-dress ambitions.) The Emanu-El Sisterhood,

I think, is a model of a relief-giving agency, in which the head and heart operate in perfect balance.

The Council brought every sort of personality into its fold, people of the aggressive organizing type, of the modest retiring sort, women who were lukewarm about their religion, women who were intensely religious, members of the old families, and some of the latest comers to America.

Mrs. Isabella Freedman, for instance, has an intensity of religious feeling such as I have seldom encountered, and it is natural that when the Council was organized her strong devotion to her people and her faith should have made her one of the first to join.

Mrs. Julius Beer, the mother of a large family, is a fine representative of one of the old German-Jewish families, the Walters, who could have boasted a coach-and-pair, having come to America and grown well-to-do decades before the immigrations of the 'eighties. Her parents were members of Temple Emanu-El when it worshipped on the second floor of a house on Second Avenue.

The situation in the New York section required delicate handling, owing to the dissension among the factions. As president I was acceptable to both sides. While my personal leanings were toward progressive Judaism, the fact that I was Alexander Kohut's widow gave me the approval of the Conservatives.

As soon as I could get my bearings, and after many conferences with Gustav Gottheil and H. Pereira Mendes, representing the two factions, I called the first meeting of the board of trustees and invited the Jewish Board of Ministers to be present. There were many questions to be settled, and many heated discussions might be expected before we could commence work of a constructive nature. I endeavored to be fair to both sides. After all, we were and wished to be known as children of Israel, and I felt that the principles of each of us was a matter of individual concern. Whether Orthodox or Conservative or Reform, we could meet upon the common ground of social service. As we expected tolerance from the Christian world, we could, by the same principle, be tolerant toward each other.

The Board of Ministers were patient and kind. I fear, though, that they may have been a bit sceptical. Perhaps they thought the future of Judaism was sufficiently safeguarded by the rabbis of the country. But they realized, I know, that a new movement had been inaugurated, and that the Jewish women of the United States were not only prepared to take their place with the women of the world, but also would be in the forefront in congregational activities.

We planned that the first open meeting of the council should be conducted in peace. Nevertheless, it developed into a stormy debate. From the meetings of the Women's Health Protective Association I had learned the essentials of parliamentary procedure. I was by no means gentle and demure when healthy rapping of the gavel was required. Bang! Bang! Bang! "You're out of order. You, too. You, too." For the chairman to waver, would have been to jeopardize the meeting. Soon all was serene and dignified. The meeting was a success. When it was over, Esther Ruskay, whom I hardly knew, rushed forward and kissed me heartily. Dr. Kohler, ardent champion of Reform, congratulated me upon managing a difficult situation. Most of the rabbis credited me with having rabbinical training.

My first appearance among the Jewish women had not been a failure. I went home and wept—wept because Alexander Kohut was not there to share in my experiences, wept because after all I was a lonely widow.

Chapter xiv

AFFLUENCE

SO THE first year of widowhood found me busy indeed. I had not much time for reflection. Between the managing of the home, the delivering of lectures in Mrs. Schiff's drawing-room, the presidency of the New York Council, and participation in the affairs of several other organizations, my daily life seemed apportioned not by the hour but by the minute. As a tribute to Dr. Kohut's congregation, I volunteered as teacher in the Sabbath School. The pressure of work in all directions made me feel that my life had not ended, but that only a chapter of it had been closed and I was beginning a new era. My circle of acquaintances widened rapidly. I was invited to speak before many of the new Council sections, which sprang up in cities all over the country in answer to a real need.

Many friends questioned the advisability of my attempting so much public work. There were moments when I, too, wondered whether my outside interests were not overshadowing my home life. It was a period in American history when women's careers were looked upon askance.

Affluence

There was much unreasoning objection to women's public activities. But I continued as I had begun. My sisters and I had always felt that while woman's interests ought to begin at home and ought to end there, they need not necessarily confine themselves to it alone.

A number of positions were offered to me, one or two rather remunerative. But my lectures at Mrs. Schiff's home were proving financially successful and my outside work was so interesting that I wanted things to continue as they were. Though I had a lurking fear that of the two or three hundred women who attended the lectures, many came in a spirit of curiosity or perhaps pity, certainly not for literary information, and though I was quite sure the work was of no educational value, yet it was more pleasant than other methods of earning a livelihood and had more to recommend it than the editing of a social column in a Jewish weekly or the writing of a necessarily amateurish homiletic for Jewish mothers. Cheered by the encouragement of Mr. and Mrs. Schiff, and the devotion of some of my newfound friends, I determined to continue the lectures for at least another year.

In time one of my daughters became a kindergarten teacher and was able to support herself, but soon our regular source of income to the family budget, the money George earned by tutoring, was cut off.

He had been continuing his studies for the

rabbinate, begun during his father's lifetime, at Columbia University and the Jewish Theological Seminary. The question of how they were to be concluded remained to be settled, and his health had also to be taken into account.

Delicate from birth, suffering from pulmonary weakness since early childhood, he had always been a subject of concern to his parents; and we had adopted the practice of having him follow the sun, going south in the winter and north in summer. Isaac M. Wise, who was in New York at the time, visited us. He urged George to attend the Hebrew Union College of Cincinnati, but we were loath to have him identified with an institution whose teachings were so opposed to Alexander Kohut's views. So Dr. Wise, Dr. Gottheil, George, and myself conferred. The two fine, broad-minded ministers helped us to decide that perhaps a European training would be more sympathetic to his father's ideals. Besides, our family physician believed that Europe for a year or two would be better than America.

Dr. Gottheil, realizing better than myself the financial difficulties, insisted upon our accepting a small stipend from the funds of the Emanu-El Theological School—once quite active—to go toward George's European education. He overcame my scruples by citing the cases of one or two of the most prominent younger rabbis who had been sent to Europe in this way. Yet it was

Affluence

a great relief when several months later I was able to return the money.

I have never enjoyed being under obligations of this sort and have tried to avoid them as much as possible. Perhaps my efforts to provide everything for myself and my children have at times been too foolishly independent. I felt I could fight fate, carve out my own career and that of the youngsters, and carry the day against the cross currents of life, against those deep-lying, inscrutable forces which mould people willy-nilly. And so I laid out a stern path for myself to travel. I insisted upon carrying the financial burden alone. I even declined an offer from my oldest brother-in-law in San Francisco, who was in comfortable circumstances, to help me with the education and maintenance of the children.

About this time an unusual event was scheduled to take place in Washington, D. C. A movement had been under way to call a Mother's Congress to discuss the status of family life in the United States from the mother's point of view. The financial sponsor of the congress was Phoebe Hearst, famous California philanthropist, who had been a school chum of my teacher, Mary Kincaid. The honorary president of the congress was Mrs. Grover Cleveland, that charming woman whose radiant personality won the love of all American women. The active president of the congress was Rachel Foster Avery.

To my surprise I learned that my leadership in

the Council in New York had reached the ears of some of the women who were organizing the congress. I received a formal invitation to represent Jewish women at the congress and to deliver an address upon the subject of "Parental Reverence in the Jewish Home."

The invitation came at a time when I was feeling the strain of my many activities. To prepare such an address required time and concentration, which I felt I could not give it. The problem for me was how to conserve energy rather than to add new responsibilities. The subject appealed to me, and yet. . . . In an impulsive moment I wrote to the secretary of the congress that I was unable to accept the invitation and asked to be allowed to suggest some other name.

The same day I met Dr. Gottheil. He was angry at me, and insisted that I telegraph immediately requesting indulgence of a woman's privilege of changing her mind. A reply soon come, expressing pleasure at the reconsideration. Dr. Gottheil and myself discussed the subject and I set to work to study it. Its importance grew on me, and I worked on it enthusiastically. Dr. Gottheil assured me I was performing a genuine mission. I rewrote the paper several times and submitted each draft for his approval.

In my father's home parental reverence had been the natural and accepted course. I remember his telling us of a great rabbi's statement that

Affluence 211

the fifth commandment, "Honor thy Father and thy Mother," had been placed between the other commandments as a bridge between man's love of God and man's duty to man. Both in my father's home and in my husband's home the children grew up imbued with love and reverence for their parents. I have stated often from platform and pulpit that if we were to go back to the old biblical standards, the future fathers and mothers of the race would be better equipped for their responsibilities, and the integrity of the home be safeguarded.

The Congress of Mothers was attracting nationwide attention. Mrs. Cleveland presided at the first session, and Mrs. Hearst crossed the continent to attend. There was such a large gathering that the great hall over the Central Market was inadequate. The speakers were asked to repeat their addresses to the overflow meetings.

When I entered the hall I saw, seated upon the platform, Mary Kincaid. Instantly the awe I had felt in her presence when a girl came upon me again. Gone were all my worldly experience, all the maturity of the crowded years. I was not the Council president, the widow, the stepmother of eight children, the lecturer and teacher, but a San Francisco school girl, afraid to approach her principal.

Stage fright was a new experience for me. Judge Mayer Sulzberger, a splendid orator, once told me he never spoke well unless he felt very nervous before his appearance. I recalled the judge's words as my knees trembled and my teeth chattered, and I tried to convince myself that I was going to speak very well. But I di-di-di-di-di-didn't thi-thi-thi-thi-thi-think so. My stage fright came as the result of the sudden sight of Mary Kincaid, and of my having exaggerated the importance of the occasion and the weight of my responsibility. I was the only Jewess on the three-day programme. Suppose the audience, which seemed entirely Christian (later I learned this was not so), found the address not worthy of the meeting. Suppose I did not prove a fitting representative for my sister Jewesses. It was not until after I had commenced and heard the sound of my voice that I gained courage. I believe that my extemporaneous speeches have always been better than my set ones. I had only read a few words when, inspired by the scene, I laid the paper down and departed from the written address, though not from the subject.

After tracing Biblical reasons for parental reverence, I told my audience that when the Jew was driven from the Temple and walked out into the world, he soon found that Christians locked him up behind ghetto walls, visible and invisible. They robbed him of the right to nearly every pursuit. All they left him was his home and the right to study the law. So he learned to value the only possessions he had and the love of the home and the respect of children for their par-

Affluence

ents were not only fostered but accentuated. Therefore, I concluded, I, as a Jewess, thanked those who had deprived us of so much that we might have contributed, because in doing so they preserved and strengthened the love of parents for children and the respect of children for their parents, which is a peculiarly Jewish virtue.

I resumed my seat amid applause, and was thanked by Mrs. Cleveland for my address. But neither Mrs. Hearst nor Mary Kincaid approached me, though they had congratulated the previous speakers.

What was the applause to me, then? I feared I had not done well, and Mary Kincaid did not approve of me, and Mrs. Hearst was angry. As soon as the morning session was over, I hurried to my hotel, even neglecting to attend the White House luncheon to which the speakers were invited. Once more lonesomeness came upon me, and I bemoaned the difficulty of doing everything alone. I had the wonderful help of kind friends, but I needed that great moral inspiring influence which Alexander Kohut had been.

A few minutes later there was a knock at the door—Mrs. Hearst's coachman bringing a large bunch of violets from his mistress and a note from Mary Kincaid: "God bless you, Rebekah, I'm proud of you. Mrs. Hearst and I will be over soon." When they came in, I fell upon Mary Kincaid's shoulder and wept. She hadn't suspected that Mrs. Alexander Kohut was her one-time pupil, and had been so startled and dumbfounded that she failed to greet me.

My address was translated into many languages and distributed throughout the world. I received a letter from the secretary of the Congress informing me that at the request of the Empress of Japan it had been translated into Japanese. Thus, in a measure, recognition had come to me through my first appearance before a non-Jewish audience.

At the Congress I had the pleasure of meeting the Rev. Anna Howard Shaw and Susan B. Anthony, two of the greatest of American women. Dr. Shaw expressed considerable interest in my address, and asked me why the Jewess had not emerged from the home and taken up her position with the others of her sex in fighting for women's rights. I was glad I could inform her of the recent organization of the Council and the remarkable progress already made. Her face shone.

Of course, I placed no great value upon the literary qualities of this or any other address, but I did decide that if the Christian world could hear what we had to say, it would serve to bring a better understanding between Jew and Gentile. So I determined that no longer would I regard my personal interest but would also accept opportunities to appear before Christian audiences.

Later I was asked to address the pupils of the fashionable and exclusive Ely School. I could see that these lovely girl pupils giggled when I was presented as a Jewess. I was determined to have my revenge, and in my talk made them so homesick for their parents that they wept. Then I told them part of the story of Heine's *Princess Sabbath* and the *Rabbi of Bacharach*, in which the ghetto Jew carries the burden typical of his race through the ages. On Sabbath eve, returning from the synagogue and entering his little home, he finds the table set with snowy cloth and lighted candles and the Sabbath bread, and becomes transformed not only in figure but in face. The bowed shoulders straighten, light enters his eyes. Is he not then a Prince of Israel, and is not his home a palace? The girls giggled no more at mention of "Jew."

One of the meetings I was asked to address was the Women's Christian Temperance Union. Obviously their idea of a Jew or Jewess had been built upon the sort of misinformation common to people who live remote from the world, as most of them did. They were one more confirmation of my father's statement that people with only a smattering of knowledge readily believe the fantastic. To these women, wholly unacquainted with Jews, it was a revelation to come face to face with a Jewess who had neither distorted features nor spoke a distorted language. Their imagination, fed on bizarre pictures and grotesque literature, had led them to expect a caricature.

Miss Ely and the Women's Christian Temperance Union both wanted to remunerate me. I refused a fee. I always felt that it would be exploitation of my religion and my Jewishness to be compensated for expounding my favorite subjects to Christian audiences. The once or twice in my life that I tried speaking for pay, I was an utter failure. Being at my best as an extemporaneous speaker, the thought that I was speaking for hire put a damper on my eloquence. To be paid for teaching seemed right, but not to plead the cause of Judaism, especially before Christians. Love of one's faith, and devotion to the cause of one's people, should be worth a sacrifice. During all the years when the family budget was so puny, I never accepted emolument for public addresses.

While pursuing his studies in Berlin, George became critically ill. Taking the two younger daughters I went abroad to be with him. In Berlin we were met by three of his fellow-students, Dr. Paul Rieger, Dr. Hermann Vogelstein and Dr. Samuel Posnanski, all of whom won renown later for scholarship.

The next three months were spent in nursing George and bringing back his strength. We left him reluctantly, but more or less consoled that he was to have the loving care and devotion of Moritz Steinschneider and his wife, who did all they could for him, and drew him into the family group not only because they had known his father,

Affluence

but also because of their deep personal affection for the son.

Professor Steinschneider was world-renowned as a bibliographer, and was known locally as one of the characters of Berlin's academic circles. There were many anecdotes in circulation about him, for one thing that he had worn the same overcoat for forty years. During my stay in Berlin he received an honorary professorship at the age of eighty. The university named a distinguished committee to make the presentation. At the head of it was Mommsen, Germany's greatest historian. But Professor Steinschneider was nowhere to be found. Finally they discovered him in a corner of the Königliche Bibliothek, engrossed in an ancient tome. With great formality they presented him with the parchment. "Ah, yes, thank you," the venerable scholar said, wondering what all the fuss was about, and returned to his reading. He stuffed the paper in his overcoat pocket, and then completely forgot about it. His wife, whom I had nicknamed George Eliot because she looked like her, found the honor certificate late in the afternoon as it fell out of his pocket, and cried: "Moritz, why did you not tell me you had become a professor?"

"I forgot," was his reply.

We were often invited to tea at the Steinschneiders' and spent many happy evenings laughing over quaint stories told by or about him.

From Berlin we went for the remainder of the

summer to Reichenau, a beautiful health resort near Vienna. Here my son recuperated wonderfully. The little hotel at which we stayed for many weeks was built almost into the mountain, and surrounded by a fragrant pine forest.

An experience I had there made our vacation a never-to-be-forgotten one.

It was the first Friday evening of our stay. As we sat on the veranda chatting with the innkeeper, we saw a man approaching from the road who looked uncommonly like my husband. He was tall; perhaps not as tall as Alexander Kohut, but of imposing stature; his face spoke eloquently of the man's soul and self-command. He had very white skin, large blue eyes, and a blue-black beard, neatly trimmed. I started as if I had suddenly seen an apparition of my husband, though a changed one.

He ascended the steps of the veranda and greeted the landlord, who turned to me and presented, "Dr. Theodor Herzl," the great prophet of Israel who had founded the Zionist movement and fired the imagination of his people with his conception of a Jewish state, who sought to make his dream reality, and traveled throughout the world in an endeavor to enlist the sympathy and support of monarchs and governments.

He had come to pay his weekly visit to his parents, who were spending the summer at Reichenau. His fame had already spread over the whole globe, and the Zionist movement was grow-

Affluence

ing with amazing rapidity. I had heard and read so much about his personality and his book *The Jewish State*, which so revolutionized the thought of Jews everywhere, that I considered it an almost sacred privilege to be able to discuss these things with the man himself. He presented me with a copy of his book and spoke quietly of the progress of his work.

At the time of my meeting with Herzl I was not in sympathy with the founding of a Jewish State. I was an ardent American, almost chauvinistic in my patriotism for the land of my father's adoption. In conversation with the Zionist leader, I told him that my husband's grandfather had gone to Jerusalem to spend the last of his life and had been buried by the wall there, and I also spoke of the yearnings of Alexander Kohut to live and die in the Holy Land.

"Speaking for myself," I continued, "I should like to visit Palestine, but I should want to be assured of a round-trip ticket."

Instantly I realized the bad taste of what I had said. To disagree was honest and fair enough, but my remark was tantamount to a sneer, and was in keeping with the legendary anti-Zionist statement: "I am in favor of a Jewish State if I can be appointed Jewish Ambassador to Paris." The remark caused me misery. Herzl, however, took it quietly and tolerantly.

He came to Reichenau every week-end for thirteen weeks. By the end of that time I was a

Zionist, converted by the great Herzl himself. In several walks together and many conversations, he gave me a real understanding of the solution of the problems of thousands of our persecuted brethren, and the fulfillment of the prophecy that we should be returned to the land of our fathers.

His ideas came at a time in the world's history when Jews were ripe for the espousal of them; they have become a part of world affairs and world movements. Yet it is undeniable that his personal charm aided greatly in their acceptance. Without his personality—magnetic, inspiring, but not demagogic—the cause of Zionism would not have taken root so quickly in the hearts of Jews the world over. Strangely enough, this man who developed into the leader of his people, pleading their cause before Kaiser, Sultan, Prime Minister, President, had at first been apathetic to Judaism, and his sudden emergence is one of the most fascinating and inspiring chapters in the history of his race.

A few years later, again in Europe, I was aboard a train bound for Vienna. At daybreak the train stopped at various stations outside the city and took on great crowds. It was unusually heavy traffic for that hour. I noted also that most of the passengers were Jewish men and women. I asked if anything special was going on. The man I addressed looked at me in astonishment. Did I not know, he asked, that the great Herzl was dead, and that his funeral was to take place that morning. The sad and dreadful news stunned me.

As soon as we arrived in Vienna, after seeing to my luggage, I hurried to the Herzl home to attend the service.

It was not difficult to learn where his home was. All the streets seemed to be filled with processions going there. I was fortunate enough, through presenting my card as an American and a newspaper correspondent, to enter the home and finally to join in the immediate procession of mourners. The only other American at the house was Seraphine Pisko, Secretary of the National Jewish Hospital for Consumptives.

Thousands walked to the cemetery through a human aisle two miles long, through a chain of young Zionists who stood clasping one another's hands.

One of the mourners explained the significance of the chain. "The Jews will never forget the teachings of Herzl and the service he rendered, and the chain of those who loved him must never be broken."

I despatched an account of the funeral to an American weekly.

A number of months after my return from Europe, I was to face perhaps the greatest economic crisis of my life.

It was in 1901. I had been living my same active social life. The Council of Jewish Women had held in New York its first national tri-ennial convention. It was a really thrilling event for the Jewish women from all over the United States to gather and meet as they had at the first Congress, and I was happy as a section president to welcome the national officers and delegates. But having lost touch with Council affairs during my stay in Europe, I took no great part in the proceedings. And in the course of the year, after four years of service, I resigned as President of the New York section. For one thing, I believed in rotation in office; for another, I wanted to devote more time to study.

I was invited a few months later to become the teacher of the confirmation class at Temple Emanu-El. The salary was the largest that until then had ever been offered to a teacher of a Jewish religious school. I do not know whether it was the compliment paid me, or the lure of the compensation, or both which led me to accept, but accept I did. I felt that here was a real mission to perform, in trying to instil a love for Judaism in adolescent girls.

So I mapped out my work with great care.

I broke up whatever group cliques existed, all the snobbish tendencies and class consciousness, by seating children acording to size, whether or not the sexton's daughter happened to come next to the girl of the wealthiest family. Many of these pupils of mine later became interested in civic welfare work, and it was a pleasure to meet them and feel that their generous devotion to the less

Affluence

fortunate could perhaps have had their beginnings during those Sunday mornings at Temple Emanu-El.

And now the crisis came.

My mother and sisters, who had been living in Richmond, returned at this time to Baltimore. I visited them and learned that a tremendous problem faced us. A bad investment had swept away their meager capital and also a considerable part of the small Kohut estate.

Somehow I felt I must not only make good to my children the money lost through no fault of my own, but determined that I must also take up the responsibilities of my mother and sisters. My father and brother were gone, and I saw myself taking their place as the breadwinner.

When I returned to New York, I spent the hours in anxious thought. The wakeful nights were dedicated to a number of schemes whereby I might earn enough to replace at least the interest lost to the Kohut estate and to assist in the maintenance of the family in Baltimore.

Why had God put it upon me to assume so much responsibility? I stood at Alexander Kohut's grave and said the burden was greater than I could bear.

There were, besides, difficulties other than economic, such as always arise in the managing of a large family. I had long since learned that without my husband I had not the same confidence in the management of the children that I had enjoyed while he was alive.

Volunteer service was now precluded. The joy of feeling I was rich enough to give myself was to be denied me.

I went to Jacob H. Schiff, and in my inexperience, shall I say youthfulness, I asked him if he could not invest our meager capital so that we could have larger returns. He assured me that he never did a thing of that sort for anyone. He told me I could sleep soundly in the knowledge that Alexander Kohut's money was invested in four per cent gold bonds.

Now that we were once more face to face with poverty, I wanted it not to gnaw too much or even at all. Egotistically sensitive, I was ashamed to tell the children that part of our money had been lost; money which had been left to me as a sacred trust. There was not even the comfort of discussing it with my oldest son, with whom I might have established another secret. He was in Europe.

But no bewailing what could not be helped. Something had got to be done. The whole question was—what? I cast about and cast about in my mind for some good plan. I rehearsed my capacities. Not writing for newspapers, not lecturing. Teaching, perhaps. Yes, teaching. My life, in a sense, had been a preparation for it. Since acquiring a teacher's diploma, I had never quite left the schoolroom atmosphere. I under-

Affluence

stood children, had studied pedagogy, and there was my experience with Dr. Kohut's Sunday-school and the confirmation class of Temple Emanu-El.

Teaching in itself, however, was not highly remunerative.

The thing to do was to start a school!

Once more I went to Mr. Schiff and told him of my plan. I told him that though the need for money was the mainspring of my ambition, the school was not to be conducted for that end alone. I pledged myself to give girls the best education New York offered and all the moral and spiritual training of which I was capable. He asked for time to consider the matter before advising me. Walking through the park, after I left his home, the notion came to me, somehow, that he intended to give me the benefit of a good investment.

A few days later he called upon me, and gave the plan his unbounded approval. He had inquired into all its features, saw that there was need for such a school, and advised me to go ahead.

I was a little resentful at the time that he did not offer to aid me financially. I felt burdened with responsibilities, and somehow entertained the fantastic notion that Mr. Schiff would throw a bag of gold at my feet and encourage me to lead a life of luxury.

Under all circumstances, however, his approval of a plan meant that I must carry it out, whatever the difficulties. Almost immediately I commenced visiting schools, studying curricula and text-books, and drawing up a prospectus. Through my class at Temple Emanu-El I made efforts to obtain a few private pupils. The Council sections, too, were informed of my project.

Soon the last series of lectures under Mrs. Schiff's auspices were under way. The subject was "Dreamers of the Ghetto," inspired by Israel Zangwill's book. This helped me to increase the income and contribute in a small way to the support of my mother and sisters.

In February of that year there was alarming news from Berlin about my son's health. School or no school, I left for Europe to be with him, engaging a secretary to take care of correspondence concerning the school, which I hoped to open in October. It was pleasant to know that many applications had been received.

My son had been removed to a health resort at Meran, near the Italian border. When I reached Meran, the oldest of the Kohut boys, the sacred heritage left me by my husband, was lying at the point of death from double pneumonia. I made desperate efforts to secure the best physicians from Vienna. A day and night vigil followed. At last he pulled through.

The Kohut School for Girls, in its formative stages, had the advantage of excellent counsel. Dr. Henry Leipziger and Julia Richman, both educators of great experience, gave an enthusiastic

Affluence

novice the benefit of their seasoned knowledge; and through their aid teachers with desirable qualifications were secured, and many pitfalls avoided.

Upon my return to New York, I again applied myself to organization, perfecting all the groundwork of management. A building was secured in West Fifty-eighth Street, with our own apartment a few doors away. In addition to providing maintenance for our family and a vocation for me, the school was to provide a partial outlet for George's abilities. With physical resources inadequate for the strenuous duties of a large congregation, he could give classes the benefit of his training without ill effect, and thereby provide a competence for himself.

The time approached for the opening of the school, and I was busied with a thousand details. It was a very tired but happy woman who sat in her office that afternoon, her dream translated into action, her school functioning at last. In the various class-rooms throughout the building, one hundred pupils who had been entrusted to her care were becoming acquainted with their teachers.

As I sat there, happy for my task in the immediate present but also wondering what the future held in store, a card was brought in. Jacob H. Schiff.

He came to congratulate me upon my venture.

"I have watched your progress," he said, "and I am delighted that you have done what you wanted to do." Then he laid a check upon my desk. "I hope you will not feel offended. Until now I would not have dared to offer you money, because I knew you wouldn't accept it. But now you are in a business venture, and that is different. Please take this as a loan for an indefinite period, to tide you over financial worries."

He walked quickly out, before I could answer. I picked the check up. It was for $10,000. A few months before I had been resentful at his apparent unwillingness to ease my financial struggles. Now I felt how untrue that resentment was to the best that was in me. Was it not finer that I had consummated my wish through my own efforts, and was not Mr. Schiff's loan doubly sweet in its compliment to my ability to help myself? What a wonderful first day for my school! That evening I walked up Fifth Avenue with the check and a note expressing my deepest gratitude, and left them at the Schiff house.

Busy days followed. The pedagogic machinery functioned well. My teachers took complete charge of the general education. I assumed as my special responsibility the girls' religious instruction. To communicate my own religious enthusiasm to my pupils was my aim, and I did not count my work well done, unless, in addition to knowledge of the Bible and ceremonial observance, I instilled into them certain moral and ethical standards which would strengthen them for the future. And so I tried to make religion so significant and

Affluence

beautiful and stimulating to the imagination that the young girls whose lives had been entrusted to me might be stirred to the soul. In my efforts I reached new outposts of my own soul. While expounding certain subjects, new vistas were suddenly flung open to me, too. The view was thrilling.

As there were both boarding and day pupils, I had not only class-room work to manage but also a household on a large scale with high standards. On Friday evenings we had religious services for resident pupils. My son presided at the services, and I blessed the Sabbath lights in the fashion of the true mothers of Israel. Friday evenings we often succeeded in recapturing the spirit of joy that had prevailed in our home in the San Francisco days; we sang and told stories and filled the hours to the brim with merriment and healthy laughter. Saturday mornings I attended services with the girls at one of the temples, and the morning of the following day I held classes in Jewish history. Happy those Sunday mornings, as I recall them.

Because of his years at the University of Berlin, George was qualified to teach German; he also taught history, which had been one of his major subjects at Columbia. I conducted a class in current events, taught English literature, and now and then substituted in mathematics, which had always been my favorite subject in school.

Once the assistant principal asked me to take a

class in geometry in place of the teacher who was ill. Fortunately I had an hour in which to prepare. The problem happened to be one that had been a stumbling block to my classmates in San Francisco days. It came to me in a moment. My success with the geometry class in that one period led me to undertake teaching mathematics regularly the next season.

As time went by and I grew more experienced in school management, I was in a state of perpetual dissatisfaction with results. Perfection was what I strove for and as there is no point in education where one can say that the summit has been reached, it was a continuous effort. Meanwhile, the standards of the institution rose and rose. I visited the best schools of the country to observe their methods, and attended classes in pedagogy at New York University. "Keeping school" was by no means easy. There were exacting parents who would have been dissatisfied under any circumstances, because it was their nature to be dissatisfied. There were unappreciative pupils. What institution is without them? I spent sleepless nights.

There were other troubles. From the moment the school was started and commanded my entire attention, my family felt neglected. Their apartment was only a few doors away, but they saw little of me, and their feeling of neglect grew into resentment. There arose a conflict of interests, which troubled not only my children but myself.

Affluence

Valerie and Margaret were both married during the five years of the Kohut School for Girls. The weddings were celebrated in the school building. Dr. Isaac Adler and Mr. Schiff attended both ceremonies and Dr. Gottheil served as the officiating minister. I mention these men particularly because, as I look back upon the past thirty years, I realize that the friends of my husband and of the early years of my life in New York were associated in after years with the important events of my life and that of my family; and until their deaths the friendship remained unbroken.

There were but four children left at home. And there were about one hundred girls whose parents were paying me for the things they had a right to demand. To supply these things required my complete absorption. It was ironic that this enterprise which I had launched for the sake of my family's maintenance should be instrumental in keeping me from them. My children —mine, in the spiritual sense—realized that I had become a slave to the new work. Before the opening of the school, though I had been occupied, I could do as much or as little as I pleased, and often in my own hours. Now I was in constant harness and almost a stranger to my dear ones. George through ill health had dropped out of the school work, and the others felt hurt.

Five years had gone by and the Kohut School for Girls was firmly established, but perhaps I should have taken a longer road to prosperity. Perhaps the time had not yet come when I could relinquish my hold upon the Kohut family. I felt pressure from without and from within, and my conscience troubled me not a little. It was pleasant enough for me to know I had rescued my mother and sisters from poverty. It was a triumph to know that I had replaced the money lost to the Kohut estate. It was satisfying to know I was a success. But then, feeling I would rather lose my school than my children, I gave up the school.

This was the greatest personal sacrifice I had been called upon to make. To many it might seem that there could have been no greater sacrifice than the original one involved in my marrying a widower with eight children. But marriage to Alexander Kohut was no sacrifice. His love was to me the greatest good fortune, and while he lived nothing seemed a burden, and the management of a large household and the active fostering of the children had far more pleasurable than distasteful elements. In later years, in harassing moments, alone with my troubles, without Alexander Kohut's great spirit to comfort and encourage me, I was assailed by doubts, and questioned the wisdom of what I had done, not only from a selfish standpoint but because of the family itself.

Observing such an abnormal married life as mine, friends have often wondered whether I did not miss having a child of my own. To that I could not answer "Yes" or "No" flatly. In my own childhood days I had witnessed the problems of stepmotherhood from the inside. I loved these children of Alexander Kohut, and decided I would try to establish a relationship as close as possible to that between a mother and her own children. Were I to have a child of my own, beside these stepchildren, mother love would come between me and the others, I should inevitably show the preference, and the family atmosphere would be inharmonious. So I elected undivided stepmotherhood rather than a divided motherhood.

My love for these children, who were not of my flesh and blood, as great as if they had been, meant not simply smiling approval when things went well, but worrying over their trials; it meant anxious, sleepless nights when there was ill health, and a deep concern over their spiritual development and material progress.

The mother-sorrow that comes when the fledglings are grown and the nest deserted was mine, too. One after another the boys and girls went their various ways. Sometimes in later years, when the home was emptied, I have thought that perhaps I was over-conscientious in having deprived myself of the satisfaction and joy of having my very own child. But the thought left me as quickly as it came. The boys and girls have grown up; have boys and girls of their own, and the relationship between us of mother and children still remains, a very real relationship, not one of lip recognition.

I think that my course was wise and right. After all, I had intruded upon these children when I joined their family, and it was my duty to be as good to them as I could.

In opening the school I thought for the first time of my own economic independence. I foresaw that in a few years the hearth would be deserted, and the school would almost be like a family on a larger scale. The school and the home were always complementary in my mind; I was a teacher in the home, and a mother in the school.

More than this, I wanted a real vocation.

My public work, while it satisfied me and helped me to live through the years of darkness, did not seem like a real profession. The school was something solid and substantial, *and* a career. Moreover, it met a religious need of mine. Often recalling my years of doubt and irreligion, I exulted that I had not only found peace and strength in the faith of my fathers, but that I could communicate that faith to others who were groping as I had done in years gone by.

However, the school was sold.

The financial returns were satisfactory. And still I was not free of the pictures still haunting me from the old days of the Fruit and Flower Mission, reinforced by later impressions of the East Side in New York—families of eight or ten living in sub-cellars, in two small rooms, dirty,

Affluence

underfed children, fine old Talmudic scholars standing at the street corners, peddling shoe-laces. My father had made a great virtue of poverty, and one of my sisters would often say: "Well, one needn't be rich to be happy." But *I* never felt the glory of poverty when I thought of the men of intellect and talent—writers, musicians, artists, philosophers—of whom there were so many on the East Side and who suffered the gnawing pangs of hunger when they might be helping to make the world a better place to live in. No, poverty had no charms.

Not that I and the four children under my roof, three boys and Elsie the youngest, were in want of anything. But the Bettelheims were still insecure. I determined that if I could help it, this should not be so. We should all be secured, freed, if possible, for always from the fear of economic cares. And over and above selfish wishes for myself and my family was a great desire to be able to pass on some of the world's goods to others. While the personal struggle had been too great, I could harbor no such ambition, but now that the school had left me with a substantial bank account of thousands where before there had been only single dollars, why not tens, even hundreds of thousands? I would do it. I thrilled to the idea again of overcoming seeming impossibilities.

On the advice of a hard-headed business man, a friend of my husband, I bought a house and took a mortgage on it. Before long the miracle happened. I had a chance to sell the house, clear the mortgage and make $5000. Until then I had invested in only gilt-edge securities. I now studied bonds bringing in larger returns, a fascinating pastime, I confess. I invested in them and increased our income. At about this time, too, one of my sons-in-law to whom I had given my share of the Kohut estate for a business enterprise of his, offered me an interest in the business. All this combined meant affluence.

In a material way, therefore, I have reached my goal. I want no more than I have. Enormous wealth I have never craved. I am independent. I have means. I can in a small way help others with my means. My children, even George, who once suffered such ill health, are comfortably established.

So the great stalking enemy of my childhood, Poverty, was vanquished, and by what strange and devious ways!

Chapter XV

RIVERDALE

FOR a year or two after giving up the school I did not take up a definite occupation. And I was sensitive about it, I shrank when my friends, as they often did, asked me: "What are you doing now?" The only answer I'd find would be: "Just playing."

Yet I was a busy woman. The family interests had widened. The married daughters had children, and there were their *family* problems to consider, too, and take to heart. In addition, I joined several classes at Columbia University as auditor, and took courses at the School of Philanthropy, and became, at Dr. Gottheil's instance, a trustee of the Emanu-El Sisterhood.

What a far cry back it seemed to me to the old days of the Fruit and Flower Mission in San Francisco, when people who needed bread were given kind words and fruit and flowers. The Emanu-El Sisterhood provided the bread, also work and kind counsel, and a day nursery for the babies of the neighborhood, and lunches for the poor children in the school on the opposite side of the street.

At the Sisterhood I learned not to give impulsively, as I had been happy to do, but to help understandingly in accordance with the newer methods, which were opposed to indiscriminate alms-giving and aimed for a proper, scientific, constructive administration of relief.

Indeed the whole system of Jewish charity has changed completely during the period of my residence in New York. Within thirty-seven years I have seen practically every Jewish institution discard its old ramshackle quarters and house itself in a palatial structure with perfect equipment. The philanthropic work of the Jews of New York has been recognized and acclaimed the world over, and the physical growth of their works has been attended by a corresponding growth of technical knowledge of their social problems. My one regret is that thirty years ago they did not realize the spiritual need of the immigrants, as to-day they realize the claims of physical distress.

There was one sweet, fine woman at the Sisterhood who as long ago as that was aware of the spiritual claims of the immigrants. So early in the communal life of the American Jewess she felt the need for drawing from the experience of her Christian friends. Though a well-to-do woman, Mrs. Celia Borg—Saint Cecilia I called her in all reverence—had much sorrow in her life. And she had the wisdom and greatness of soul that sorrow sometimes gives.

It may seem odd that I should have allied

myself with a Sisterhood not connected with my husband's congregation. For one thing, the sight of his vacant chair depressed me. And then I felt myself identified with all synagogues instead of with one. As a matter of fact, for several years, I scarcely attended any synagogue at all. George and I read prayers together at home—led by an invisible spiritual chief whose memory was sacred to us.

George, thoroughly educated, a scholar loving scholarship, and imbued with the idea of carrying on the Kohut tradition, was eager to follow in his father's footsteps. But his ambitions were constantly endangering his health. The duties of a rabbi of a Dallas congregation, which he assumed for a time, proved too much for his frail physique; he even had to give up librarianship at the Jewish Theological Seminary. The thought of idleness and dependence upon me, however, was abhorrent to him, and we discussed the question of his future, again and again.

Oddly enough, the solution to his problem was the same as it had been to mine.

A school.

He decided to establish a private school and summer camp for boys. That was in 1907.

We chose for the location of the school Riverdale-on-the-Hudson, convenient to New York, of which it is really a part, and yet remote and lovely. To me the Hudson is most beautiful there, at the turn north of Manhattan and Spuyten Duyvil, where you can almost fancy yourself at the Lake of Lucerne, with the Palisades rising on the opposite shore and the trees reflected dark and green in the slow-moving water.

The house we selected was a solid mansion, with walls two feet thick, built, we were told, to be the home of the Babcocks, an old New York family, for succeeding generations. The lawns, planted with a variety of great trees, sloped down to the very edge of the Hudson.

As the school was George's, and he made a success of it—it gave him a career and an income—this, I feel, is the place for me to speak of him at length. I have scarcely done more in the latter part of this record, than refer to his health which, by the way, improved tremendously. He has been a stronger man ever since he went to Riverdale.

One can imagine that the executive work in connection with the school was a task in itself. But in addition to that and to actual teaching, George also found time to do considerable writing. A list of his publications would fill several pages.

He has won recognition as an able student of Semitic lore, and though he never attempted his father's prodigious works in this field, it was his father who was his inspiration. George sought not so much gratification on his own account as to be able to do things that he might dedicate to his memory—a tribute to the great love that Alexander Kohut inspired in his children.

Riverdale

Alexander Kohut had wanted to do so many things for Jewish scholarship which perhaps in his heart he realized he would never be able to do. The only codicil to his will was an expression of hope that we would be able, each anniversary of his death, to help a poor student. This we have done every year. More recently, George's material prosperity having increased somewhat, he dedicated the greater part of his none too large income to create Alexander Kohut Foundations at Yale University, the Vienna Seminary, in Berlin, and at the Jewish Institute of Religion, over which that famous pupil of my husband's, Stephen S. Wise, presides. These foundations provide for the publication of Semitic studies of recognized value. Alexander Kohut had known what it meant for a scholar to be denied the opportunity of publication, and his family knew what sacrifices he had had to make. Beside his *Aruch Completum* other manuscripts gathered dust for years before they found a publisher.

In 1912 Yale University was the recipient of the Alexander Kohut Memorial Collection—several thousand volumes of Oriental and Semitic literature, including many valuable sixteenth-century prints and rare manuscripts and books of every description. The collection is especially rich in early editions of the Bible and its commentaries, Talmudic and rabbinic literature, standard lexica, and other reference works. A complete file of the most important periodicals in Hebrew and modern languages, many now exceedingly scarce, are a feature of the collection, which has been augmented from time to time by George, who has ever been on the lookout for books worthy to add to the original collection.

The Alexander Kohut Memorial Publication Fund was instituted in October, 1915, as the combined gift of the family and the University. This made possible the continuation of the Yale Oriental Series, comprising texts and studies in Assyrian, Babylonian, Hebrew and Arabic literature, with occasional special monographs on historical and ethnological subjects. A number of important volumes have already appeared, among them Dr. F. H. Lutz's *Early Babylonian Letters from Larsa* and Professor A. T. Glay's *The Empire of the Amorites*—the latter based upon a fresh investigation which definitely disposes of the favorite theory of the Arabian origin of the Semites.

The twenty-fifth anniversary of my husband's death was marked by the establishment at Yale of the first Semitic fellowship at an American college. The Alexander Kohut Research Fellowship in Semitics is awarded annually, on recommendation of the faculty, to a student pursuing investigations intended for publication, preferably a student who has already received the doctor's degree. The fellowship funds helped to meet one of the greatest needs of the Yale Graduate

Riverdale

School, which was seriously handicapped by the lack of money available for the aid of students.

The first holder of this fellowship, it is interesting to note, was a woman and a Christian, Ettalene N. Grice, Ph.D.

I look back on the years at Riverdale as on the whole years of peace, though there was plenty of the struggle of one sort or another that has always marked my life. I had, of course, nothing to do with the management of the school, and often chafed under the restrictions of many rules and the taking of orders from men teachers younger than my son. Nevertheless, there was a self-appointed task for me in which I rejoiced—being mother to young creatures again, as I had been in the Beekman Place days. I had a real vocation, a real function—something I had lacked since I gave up my own school for girls.

And then there was Grace Dodge!

To understand what it meant for me to have her as a close neighbor, I must go back many years to the days when I gave lectures at Mrs. Schiff's home, was President of the New York Section of the Council of Jewish Women, and did communal work, besides, on the Lower East Side.

As I have tried to make clear, I had long before my husband's death, turned from the doubt and irreligion of my girlhood and developed a strong, religious feeling. It made me happy that the Council gave a strong impetus to Bible study and that by getting to know religious history, Jewesses who had perhaps regretted that they were born in the faith and were carrying the Yoke of the Torah, became ardent advocates of synagogue services and ceremonial observance in the home. Women were elected to the Sabbath-School Committees of synagogues and the women it was who established religious schools among the immigrants.

I should like to pause here, if I may, and speak more of the Council and what it stands for in its thirty years of existence. Besides its valuable contributions to Jewish life, and the fact that it gave women of our faith a national outlook, its aid to immigrants, its Americanization programme, its co-operation with congregations, its efforts in the correction of social evils, its voluntary suppression of its own identity in the gathering of war relief funds for the American Jewish Relief Committee, and its considerable service in Europe during the critical post-war period, are among a few of its achievements.

As a young girl I had been an enthusiastic reader of *Young Israel*, a Cincinnati publication which had suspended. It occurred to me that the Council should conduct a Sabbath school paper, and I discussed the matter with Julia Richman. She agreed with me and we invited Professor Richard Gottheil, son of Gustav Gottheil, to join us. The little paper, the only one of its kind, was called *Helpful Thoughts*. From the start it was a decided success and received considerable encouragement. Several of the rabbis contributed, particularly my dear friend Maurice H. Harris, to whom I have always remained grateful for the help he gave me at the time. I needed the counsel of sympathetic rabbis now that both my father and husband, who could have been of tremendous aid, were gone. Dr. Harris at once established a Bible circle, the outgrowth of which was that splendid and unique contribution to religious school pedagogy, the several volumes of *The People of the Book*. It covers the entire range of Biblical and post-Biblical history, and, with its bibliography and references, formed not only splendid text-books for pupils but ideal handbooks for teachers. I think I am safe in saying that the Council of Jewish Women was indirectly the cause of Dr. Harris's having written *The People of the Book* and his subsequent histories.

But the Council could only scratch the surface. The need for religious work among the immigrant Jews of the East Side, especially of the younger generation, was tremendous, as I discovered when I came to work at the Educational Alliance soon after the erection of the big building at the corner of East Broadway and Jefferson Street, which became the intellectual centre for the Russian Jewish immigrants who had begun to arrive in waves after the persecutions of the early 'eighties.

I took over a large class in English at the invitation of Professor Edwin R. A. Seligman of

Columbia University and David Blaustein, the Superintendent of the Educational Alliance—a product of the Americanization of the immigrant, typical in the highest and finest degree. He worked his way as a lad through sweatshops to go to Brown University. And he wielded a tremendous influence among the immigrants who huddled about the Alliance. That ungraded class never failed to bring tears to my eyes and a lump to my throat—white-bearded fathers sitting beside their alert young sons, both studying the English alphabet from the same book. I wonder if there has ever been anything like it in the world's history.

That period was an intense one, intense in its suffering, in its desire for knowledge, in its struggle for economic betterment. The lot of the Orthodox Jewish immigrant was particularly hard. His religious ideals kept him from working on the Sabbath. The restrictions in Russia had prevented the Jews altogether from learning many trades. So the limitations were numerous. There were not many places where a middle-aged Jew with little skill and refusing to work on Saturday could find a job.

Aside from the actual material suffering, the situation produced many a family tragedy. The younger generation was readier to adapt itself to American conditions, and while the old folk bitterly opposed their working on the Sabbath and in general assuming the ways of the Gentiles, yet they found themselves dependent upon their children for support. It was a sad state of affairs.

At the same time there were numberless instances in which the two generations shared the same ambitions and were typical of the strong family devotion for which the Jew is famed.

Ambition. Almost the key-word to the Jewish East Side. Not a sordid ambition for worldly goods. That only in a slight degree as compared with the soaring ambition for study and knowledge and art and music. The Jewish immigrant's desire for self-improvement was so great and his circumstances so wretched, that Americans learning of it were inevitably put to shame because of their neglect of their own glorious opportunities. Slums exist in every country, but none elsewhere than in Jewish East Sides in which the people strive for the stars, thrusting aside what is ugly and base in their surroundings and filling their souls with the fine and the beautiful.

Yet not all living squalor, amid disease and vice, can find beauty in life. Each human being actually produces his own world, more or less colored by his outer circumstances. For some, not necessarily weak people, outer circumstances may be too strong for them to be able to create a desirable world. Such people need spiritual help. And none was offered to the Jewish immigrants.

The younger ones, not having had the religious training that their parents had had in European communities, found no adequate incentive here.

Most of the synagogues hastily erected for the new arrivals were located in corner stores, in unsanitary tenements, squalid and uninspiring. Communicating the religious spirit to the young in such quarters was a well-nigh impossible task. The quality of religious teaching was low, the places of instruction far from inviting, and services in unfamiliar Hebrew became more and more a barrier than a bridge to religious understanding.

Beginning with the influx of Russian and Polish Jews, the Protestant Church made a decided attempt and spent considerable money, to effect conversions. Zangwill put into the mouth of Heine: "The mission of Christianity will not be over until the Christians have been converted to the religion of Christ." But many Christians believe that Christ's mission on earth will be fulfilled when all the Jews have been converted to Christianity. Mission schools were established throughout the city, and a great many Jewish children were enrolled because their parents were ignorant of their purpose. Some children attended Jewish Sabbath-schools on Saturday and Christian Sunday-schools the next morning. A number of so-called rabbis who had been "converted" were paid high salaries to preach the Gospel. It was learned that the majority of them were neither rabbis nor converts, merely unscrupulous persons who took to converting as an easy and prosperous livelihood. For a number of years the columns of the secular press were filled with controversies engendered by these attempts at conversion.

I had discussed the subject of conversion with my husband many times, and he had explained that the synagogue placed little faith in conversion of any sort, whether from or to Judaism. History had recorded some rare cases of Jews who had been honestly converted to another faith, but on the whole, when Jews left the faith, they usually did so because they could no longer endure the suffering and torture of persecution, or because of some promised social advantage, in which case, their religion could not have been real religion, and their conversion, not real conversion.

There was no denying, however, that the provisions for Jewish religious training were deplorably bad. The pity of it was born in upon me in all its tragic significance during my participation a few years later in the campaign to elect Seth Low mayor of New York—incidentally, my first political experience.

Here is where Grace Dodge comes in.

I was associated intimately in that campaign with two of the finest types of womanhood that America has produced: Mrs. Josephine Shaw Lowell, inspirer of the Women's Municipal League and the Consumers' League, and Grace Dodge, president of the Young Women's Christian Association.

We electioneered throughout the entire city, going through the East Side tenements, penetrating dangerous alleyways, climbing to fourth and fifth floors to address men's clubs. One night we wound up a whirlwind tour at a mass-meeting of three hundred young men and women in the Church of the Holy Communion at Sixth Avenue and Twentieth Street. Shortly after we arrived a young woman approached me and said she had attended one of my classes in the Educational Alliance. I asked her about her religion. She said she had been thinking a great deal about the struggles of the Jews and the unabating prejudice against them, and being unable to endure it any longer she had become a convert to Christianity.

"There are a number of other Jewish men and women in this club who have become Christians," she informed me, and added that she knew Miss Dodge well and had come under her influence.

The blood surged in my veins. My heart pounded wildly. In less than a second I was filled with doubt as to the integrity of these women who held such a high place in my esteem. They had become more than co-workers. They were now intimate friends to whom I could take my personal troubles and go away with fresh confidence and a new lease on life.

All sorts of thoughts rushed through my brain.

Assuming outer calm I told Miss Dodge I could not address the club, because I had nothing to say. And I sat through the meeting, angry and rebellious, unable to understand why these women included conversion among their activities. Why?

Was there not enough irreligion and ignorance among the Christians to occupy the attention and tax the purse of the Churches? Would it not be more creditable to bring their own wanderers back to the fold?

After the meeting Mrs. Lowell made hurried adieus, while Miss Dodge and I departed leisurely. At the street corner I stopped, and said:

"Miss Dodge, are you making a great and concerted effort to convert Jews?"

"Until the Jews of New York," she said, "realize their religious responsibility toward their brethren of the East Side, and as long as any unchurched man or woman of any faith knocks at our doors, we shall greet them lovingly in the name of Christ."

We were launched on a discussion, but the hour was late, and I realized I had been impulsive. We agreed that we needed plenty of time for a talk of this sort, and decided to meet for the purpose soon. Meanwhile, we should continue to work together on the most amicable of terms for the election of Seth Low.

On my way home I could think of nothing but the subject that had caused me so much pain. I realized how little, in proportion, was being done for the religious education of the immigrant Jew. In the whole East Side, teeming with thousands, spiritual sustenance had to be sought by the individual himself, with no effort upon the part of the community to assist. True, the Federation of

Temple Sisterhoods and the Council of Jewish Women had some years before established Hebrew schools for children. But what was being done for adolescents and adults who had absorbed secular knowledge in the public schools, yet had neither the opportunity nor perhaps the desire to seek their God through prayer and service?

Miss Dodge and I met finally to discuss the question of conversion. I was amazed to find that she knew the Old Testament thoroughly, and was well equipped to bring knowledge to those who need the emotion which religion alone can supply. It was only the first of many meetings, in which we talked over the problems of both of us and reached a common ground of religious principle, despite our difference in creeds.

But after the campaign was over, our ways parted and we saw less and less of each other.

Grace Dodge came back into my life when I needed a friend for myself.

She lived near us at Riverdale, I found, and whenever a trouble—real or fancied—took hold of me, I could run to her with it and be healed. She was a great healer of souls. Once when I had unbosomed myself and wept on her shoulder, she said she might some day ask the same privilege of me—as if Grace Dodge could ever have personal problems! I believe she never existed in her own self-consciousness.

My troubles were mostly fancied, I suppose. From this length of time it seems difficult to make real to myself the things that agitated me then. Perhaps what was at the bottom of my mental distress was the lack of a vocation, a calling. Alexander Kohut, while he was alive, had been my *great* calling. Then had come my school. That had been taken away, and so, in a sense, had my family. The Bettelheims and the older Kohut children had been established. Nothing seemed left for me to do. I had been self-appointed leader of two families and my influence was waning. Important steps had been taken, I would hear, without my having first been consulted. Was it vainglory that had made me want to dominate? Was it wounded vanity from which I was suffering? Probably a little of the two elements entered, though if anyone can diagnose one's own case, I should say that I am one of those who can never feel satisfied in her soul nor well in her body unless she is carrying a load of real and grave responsibilities.

If it was no longer to be a Kohut or a Bettelheim who would draw upon the fount of motherly feelings in me, then it must be other people's affairs about which I must worry in the future.

To what, to whom, should I turn?

Chapter xvi

SOCIAL WORK

THE answer to the question with which the last chapter closed may seem too cold, too dispassionate to be a real solution to a very burning problem. To me, I assure you, it was as profoundly satisfying as if I had been a girl of sixteen plunging blindly into an *affaire du coeur*. It was not a lover I needed, nor another husband. Alexander Kohut had satisfied my being too profoundly for me to entertain the faintest thought of marrying again. When the possibility presented itself, as it did several times, I was utterly unmoved.

The thing I needed was work that would engage my whole heart.

I found it.

It must not be thought that in all these years of which I have been writing and telling of my personal affairs, I did not take part in any number of activities. I was always attending committee or mass meetings of one sort or another, and, to my pride and consolation, was asked to speak at public gatherings, synagogues and lecture halls. Then too, there were the Council of Jewish

Women and the Emanu-El Sisterhood, with which I have never ceased to be associated. Many years later, in fact, I had the proud distinction of being the Honorary President of the Sisterhood, in whose two-fold work of neighborhood house and administrator of charity, I have always taken the keenest interest.

My sister Cyd was for several years resident directress of the Sisterhood. She had also been first directress of the Settlement and Recreation Rooms on Orchard Street founded by the Council of Jewish Women, as I like to think, because of Grace Dodge, in response to the need on the part of our Jewish community that had been pointed out to me by that great Christian woman. I had many reasons, therefore, to be engrossed by this piece of social work. It was in itself a fine thing; it had been created by the Council, whose women might pride themselves for having so quickly taken up their share of communal and religious obligations; and it offered an opportunity to my dear sister. I had previously procured her a position in the Census Department in Washington. The family's situation in Baltimore now looked precarious, and I persuaded Cyd to come and take charge of the little tumble-down house that had once been the home of an old Knickerbocker family.

This was at the same time in the early nineties that I was teaching at the Educational Alliance. Young women in those days were not supposed to walk the streets alone, so, after class, I used to call for Cyd at Orchard Street, as she was timid, and we'd go home together. Not that Cyd need have had any fears—not in those crowded, noisy streets among our own people, miserable and poor though they were, but never ruffianly. The East Side, Hester, Essex, Delancey, Clinton, Allen and all the other streets, then had a glamour which, I believe, has worn off somewhat, the glamour of one didn't know what potentialities for America in the emanation of some great spiritual force from this race which had no real proletariat, only an intellectual and a merchant class.

However, the misery on the East Side, the squalor, the widening family breaches between the old and the young, produced a hitherto unknown phenomenon in Jewry—the wayward girl.

The house on Orchard Street was designed not for the girl who had strayed, but for the girl who worked; to keep her from temptation.

As yet there were no schools of philanthropy to guide the social worker. Cyd had to feel her way. I knew the experience she had had in our father's home, which had been open to all who needed help, would be of use to her now. But Cyd was the only one in our robust family who was frail. Her childhood illnesses had made her sensitive and shrinking. It was only the economic necessity resulting from the death of our father that drove her into the world's battles. By nature she was the last person in the world fitted for the nagging humiliations of coping with an interfering board of managers, no matter how well-intentioned and really a fine body that board of managers might be. Nevertheless she made a success at Orchard Street. She created a happy atmosphere, from which the girls got a sense of wholesome fun that cut out the craving for more exciting pleasures; and she made them feel to her as to a sister who is also a companion and a confidante.

Cyd, as a matter of fact, is an excellent example of what modern conditions make of old-fashioned types. Cyd to-day is a successful, well-to-do woman, entirely through her own efforts. She was the first to start a camp for Jewish children. Later she was joined by my sister Eva.

Eva, named after our maternal ancestress, is the only child of my little stepmother. She's a real Bettelheim—has always been from the day she was born. She looks like the Bettelheims, feels like them, acts like them. Everything was against Eva. She was so much younger than the rest, and she was in danger of being spoiled. Father's training, however, counterbalanced everything else, and probably her strong family resemblance to us kept her from being set apart. She became more of a sister to us than we to her, and when she joined forces with Cyd in the summer-camp project while still a young woman, it was her strong family devotion that partly moved her.

Of course, all sorts of girls visited the little

red house on Orchard Street—young, beautiful, frivolous, serious, "on the border line," emaciated from sweatshop work or study. Many, I found, were undergoing the same spiritual throes that I myself had in girlhood, and at the time I wondered if in their future lives there would be a further resemblance. There was.

Many have "emerged" as I have done, and gone far ahead. There was Alma Gluck, the celebrated singer with the voice of a flute, at that time a simple little dressmaker's daughter. And there was Jeanne Tonkonogy, the daughter of the proprietor of a delicatessen shop. I helped her get her first job, in a necktie factory. Today she is a lawyer, standing every chance of entering the office of the United States Attorney-General.

I may add a line here to say that the Council later did establish a home on Staten Island for wayward girls and unmarried mothers, at which the mothers are given a chance to support both themselves and their babies. It has sent many a self-respecting young woman out into the world again.

Deeply interested as I was in all the organizations with which I was connected, they did not seem to fill my life. There was still a void. A part of me had been left untouched—the girl still living in me, I think.

What came, finally, to serve as an outlet for her was a strike of working girls in New York

City. Different as my lot was from theirs, yet I felt a certain affinity with them. Girls the world over have the same emotional conflicts, the same spiritual trials, the same vague longings and aspirations. I had been poor enough in my life to know how economic misery multiplies these inner struggles.

I would help these working girls fight for bread, for decent homes, for a living wage, for the bare elementary things of life.

In those days unions had not yet secured wages of eight and ten dollars a day for laboring men. Girls were still worse underpaid. One way to help them in the regular course of things would be to see that they were taught trades. They must be lifted out of the class of "unskilled labor."

Now it happened that the Young Women's Hebrew Association invited me to become a member of its Board of Trustees. With the memory of the shirtwaist strike still in my mind, I accepted, but on the condition that I be permitted to reorganize their Employment Bureau and become its head.

It was to be several months before the Young Women's Hebrew Association was to take occupancy of its new building on 110th Street. I used the interim to study the machinery of a number of employment bureaus in the city. I also visited the factories, spoke to employers, and interviewed trade union officials. The deeper I went into the work, the more satisfied I became that I had at last found something to possess my entire being.

There is nothing so destructive to one's morale as being out of work. Had I myself not just gone through a period of disorganization because I had nothing definite to do? And *I* did not have to earn my daily bread. In earlier years it had been a dreadful ordeal for me to look for work. How it must hurt to receive rebuffs! One loses one's confidence and self-respect. Even if one has enough to eat and wear it reduces the physical vitality. Human beings depend upon work not only for sustenance but also for sanity. In counting my blessings, I recognize the desire and the ability to work as one of my greatest.

The Bureau opened in July, 1914, just as the war burst upon the world.

While we were still dazedly trying to realize that Europe was actually at war, that Russia and Germany were at each other's throats, that Belgium and France had been invaded, the first commercial backwash was felt here. The Stock Exchange was closed, thousands were thrown out of work, factories were shut down, and mercantile establishments reduced their personnel.

So far from being able to put my pet theories into execution, I considered myself fortunate if I obtained any sort of work for an applicant. By the end of September the employment bureau was crowded to suffocation; outside were hundreds of girls clamoring for jobs.

It was clear that girls who were "boarding out" would soon be without a home if they could not get work, and that girls without sufficient food would get ill. Every day something happened to point in this direction; a girl would faint and then admit that she had had no food for twenty-four hours.

We realized that something radical must be done. There were one or two organizations such as the Young Women's Christian Association and the Vacation Association which had already met the situation to some extent by serving lunches at minimum rates and establishing work-rooms paying tide-over wages. There was discussion at first whether these work-rooms broke down the standards of organized labor. But it was conceded finally that the minimum wage would be fair under the circumstances, considering that the work the women were called upon to do, the making of garments for Belgian children, was not in competition with the industries of the country. We could not grasp what was going on the first days of September. Hundreds of girls were trying to force their way into the Employment Bureau, and now and then some girl would sink down unconscious from lack of food. One or two said they had sat in the parks or roamed the streets, hoping for better luck next day.

It was at this time that the opportunity offered itself to co-operate with groups of women whose names had been those to conjure with, Anne

Morgan, who began her war service in America and ended it by rebuilding a whole district in France, Gertrude Robinson Smith, and Maude Wetmore. They had heard of our program in the Young Women's Hebrew Association and asked whether we could not work out a plan of co-operation with their associations. The rooms of the Vacation Association were crowded with Jewish girls, who were receiving as much sympathy and consideration as we were giving the Jewish girls in the upper part of the city.

One of the rich Jewish women with whom I formed a close companionship in this unemployment work was a philanthropist whom I had come to love and admire as long before as the first days of the Emanu-El Sisterhood, on the board of which she was for many years active. Mrs. Daniel Guggenheim, lovely to look at, might, like Mrs. Einstein, have been taken for a spoiled darling. But she, too, threw herself with impassioned ardor into her work and made the cause of the girls her own. She was tender in her sympathy, and has always responded with a fine willingness to any request I might make on behalf of some work with which I was connected. She was the first to give a large sum to the unemployment committee, and was followed by Mr. Schiff, Mrs. Henry Morgenthau, and Mrs. Isabella Freedman.

But even the combined forces of the various organizations were not sufficient to cope with all there was to do.

Social Work

The unemployment period of 1914-15 was perhaps the most serious and widespread that America has ever experienced. Never in the history of the United States had so many people found themselves out of work; literally hundreds of thousands were roaming the streets of New York, hungry and without shelter.

So this was my new piece of work. I, who but a few months before had yearned for occupation, found myself fairly staggering under the load that had fallen upon me. I have never suffered from lack of work since.

To me all the things I have undertaken since then have been as thrilling—forgive the abused word!—as though I had engaged in the wildest adventure. But I know it would take the greatest literary artist in the world to make them as thrilling to the reader. So I shall not even touch upon the numerous social enterprises that have filled my time in later years.

It takes real self-restraint on my part not to write at length of how our employment work spread; how I served as industrial chairman for the National League for Women's Service, with Maude Wetmore, Anne Morgan, Getrude Robinson Smith, and others, aiding Mrs. Willard Straight in making farmerettes of hundreds of New York debutantes; how I helped raise funds for the American Jewish Relief and Joint Distribution Committee; how I came to be appointed a "Dollar-a-Year" woman connected with the federal employment clearing-house instituted as a war measure; how I, representing the Jewish women of the country, was appointed by John D. Rockefeller, Jr., on a committee of the United War Work campaign along with Mrs. Henry P. Davison, representing the Protestants, and Mrs. Nicholas Brady, representing the Catholics, to tour the country and address mass-meetings and organize units, at which my slogan was "U. S. stands for United Spiritually."

Chief of all, I should like to write at length of the reconstruction work in Europe done by the Council of Jewish Women, which sent several units of women immediately after the armistice to various European ports and centres where refugees were crowding by the thousands, waiting, under conditions too dreadful to believe, to embark for America.

This overseas activity of the Council shall have a chapter to itself.

Chapter xvii

OVERSEAS ACTIVITIES

THE Council of Jewish Women, being the chief organization of Jewish women, naturally wished to serve in war work under its own auspices, believing that it should stand as a unit alongside the Young Women's Christian Association and the Red Cross. But other interests militated against it. The Jewish men felt that everything should be done through the Joint Distribution Committee and the Jewish Welfare Board. Our work was lauded, but we were asked to serve under these organizations. So the Council and its 150 (now 221) sections, suppressing the identity of its own organizations, took part in the various fund-raising campaigns of the Joint Distribution Committee.

In November, 1917, at the triennial meeting of the Council, I introduced a resolution calling for the raising of a fund to equip and send a unit of Jewish women to Europe.

The resolution was unanimously passed and a committee appointed to consult with the chairman of the American Jewish Relief Committee, Felix

M. Warburg, who gave his approval. The natural person to turn to was Felix M. Warburg. In a sense, Mr. Schiff's mantle of Elijah fell upon his shoulders. The two men are very different in temperament and yet neither of them has ever been exceeded by anyone in Israel in their devotion to Jews and Judaism. When we went to him there was no question in our mind but that Mr. Warburg would give financial assistance and secure us the co-operation of other agencies. Work was then begun to stimulate the collecting of funds throughout the various sections, but because of the great drives for Jewish war relief, for the Federation of Jewish Philanthropic Societies of New York and for the Jewish Welfare Board, the Council was each time asked to postpone its active solicitation until such campaigns were over.

When it became apparent that the overseas work for women was increasing and that there were immediate demands for women workers, the committee decided that activity should not be postponed until after the war, but that steps should be taken at once to equip and support a unit of Jewish women in the field. This was to be done if co-operation could be arranged with the Jewish Welfare Board. It couldn't, in spite of repeated conferences with officials of that body.

What a pity that an organization of women as representative as the Council should not have been *welcomed* to do its appropriate work!

However, we lent our experience and Council

machinery unstintedly to the fund-raising efforts, but were resolved to do reconstruction work under our own auspices after the war.

Long before the war was over, I foresaw reconstruction needs. My mother and myself had often discussed the work of the women of the South after the Civil War, and I recalled that there was as much to do then as during the war. It took no great effort of imagination to picture the aftermath; broken homes, scattered families, homeless orphans, refugees tramping across Europe, and huddling in masses at the ports—people so spent that they had not the strength or will to repair their fortunes themselves.

In April, 1920, the president of the Council appointed me chairman of the Reconstruction Committee and ordered me to go abroad and make a study of conditions in the various countries and determine what aid was needed.

Upon my informing Jacob H. Schiff, he gave me the first contribution towards the unit. We realized that the Council could not commit itself to any program involving large sums of money; the Joint Distribution Committee needed the whole and undivided co-operation of American Jews so far as the giving of money was concerned. Nevertheless we felt that we might make a contribution in social work that perhaps would be of lasting benefit and of greater value than any money we might spend.

So I left for Europe with my personal secretary.

We visited London, Paris, Antwerp, The Hague, Rotterdam, Berlin, Kattowitz, Vienna, Budapest and Frankfurt.

If my tears could have left an indelible imprint, they would have made a line along the streets of Europe through Cherbourg, Holland, Germany, Austria and Poland and back to France.

Everywhere one met little children who had been lost in the shuffle; mothers looking into the eyes of the lost ones in the hope of finding their own children, who had strayed from them when city after city and village after village had been evacuated. There were gaunt faces of men, who might have looked like the men of my own family had they had the same experience. Everywhere I saw my father and my brother among the Jewish scholars and students of Europe.

Sometimes there would be a wife who had waited for two years for one of those dreadful vises which seemed never to come from Washington, to make it possible for her to join her husband and children in America. In Rotterdam, sitting in the doorway of the Montefiore House, was a poor creature who stared with vacant eyes while three children tugged at her skirts. She had lost her reason through waiting two years in vain. Near Frankfurt a home had been established for some hundred children who did not know their names, having been lost before they had learned to speak.

Amid this chaos anti-Semitism was rampant.

As was usual, the classes who had made the war sought a scapegoat to divert attention from themselves; and the Jew—already bowed and broken from his sufferings—proved a convenient one.

Jews were massacred in the Ukraine, harassed in Poland, driven in refugee bands from place to place—a starving, footsore, weary-eyed army. The Asyl of Paris was filled with refugees; yet the misery was mild compared with the tented colonies in Belgium and the overcrowded quarters and whole districts in the German and Austrian cities. None of these unfortunates had desired to halt at these various places and make themselves dependent upon the bounty of their co-religionists, but they were not in a position to help themselves. The local philanthropic organizations were doing everything within their power, but their resources were limited.

The Jews of Antwerp rented a large plot of ground and raised vegetables for the refugees, teaching them how to cultivate the patch.

Twenty thousand refugees were living in tents at the Hague, besides a number who were quartered in the Montefiore Home in Rotterdam, in what had once been a palace, given by the Dutch government as a shelter for transient emigrants. The building was crowded, and the great neglected garden, knee-high with weeds, was full of tents, with thousands waiting almost hopelessly for a steamship to carry them away from the scenes of their sorrows. All were dejected, and there was no effort to give them an occupation to lighten their minds while they waited.

Among the transmigrants at Rotterdam, I found a young man who could speak English very well. He had left the United States to fight for Poland, but when he saw how the nation oppressed minorities, particularly his co-religionists, he left in hatred. I urged him to organize classes in English, so that the people who were waiting would lose no time in learning the language of their future land. A week after my arrival I experienced the joy of listening to a well-trained chorus singing *My Country, 'tis of Thee*. The plan of starting the process of Americanization in Europe had been discussed in newspapers, but this was the first time I had seen it in operation, and it was a source of gratification to know it had been instituted through my efforts. The idea has since been put into general practice.

In Antwerp and Berlin we found the Zionists doing useful work in conjunction with several other local organizations. The Zionist organizations of Europe filled me with awe and admiration. They were perhaps the only group that had a real programme at that time, and the inspiration of the programme gave them tremendous energy, though their funds were limited. Ten employment exchanges for refugees were maintained in Germany through funds contributed by the Zionists, the German-Jewish Hilfsverein, and the Joint Distribution Committee. The central bureau in Berlin was so efficiently conducted, and its records were so admirably kept, as to make the Federated Employment Bureau in New York jealous.

We were advised in Berlin to visit Kattowitz and observe the misery among the individuals huddled in the refugee camps there. This town on the German-Polish border was the seat of such distress as I had never seen before. Yet the soul of Judaism lived even in these surroundings. For instance, I saw an old man teaching a very small boy to read the Bible. They were grandfather and grandson; the rest of the family were dead. The old man had not much longer to live, and his one wish was that the boy should know the Book. In Germany we were told that 70,000 Jews had fled from Poland to Germany since the armistice, most of them entering by way of Kattowitz.

Wherever we went in Europe we heard of the remarkable work of Frau Anitta Müller in Vienna, where conditions were perhaps worst of all. Tens of thousands of refugees had entered the city, which lacked food even for its normal population. In Antwerp they had told us of her; in The Hague; in Berlin. And finally we met Frau Müller herself. Through her efforts 25,000 refugee Jews were being supported. First she had given of her own income; this being inadequate, she had secured other aid. And what a variety of relief institutions she had established; canteens, lying-in-hospitals, day schools, nurseries, a clinic for ailing children, trade schools for girls and women (with 5,000 pupils), and an orphan asylum. When resources proved insufficient, she levied taxes on people's incomes. She commenced with the wealthiest. In a circular she explained that, since the state levied a percentage tax for the carrying on of its administrative functions, she too would impose a stipulated monthly sum for the remainder of the war. She went straight through the various grades of affluence, down to those from she asked two crowns, in pre-war currency about forty cents a month. So she succeeded in making her work grow and pay for itself.

Everywhere I asked the people in charge of relief what they thought was the best thing the Council could do for them. The almost invariable reply was that we should send our social workers —fresh, energetic, and undiscouraged—and let them initiate measures which would both ameliorate the conditions of the refugees and demonstrate methods to the Europeans.

I put the same question at the annual convention of the Deutscher Frauenbund, representing more than two hundred women's organizations and held in the little city of Elberfeld, on the Rhine. The president of the Frauenbund, my friend, Bertha Pappenheim, invited me to attend.

I shall not forget the expressions of surprise when the German women learned from Fräulein Pappenheim that an American woman had come to see them and help them if possible; and that

Overseas Activities 273

this American woman was the daughter of a rabbi, the wife of a rabbi, the mother of a rabbi. They held back a moment timid and aloof; then one came forward and said: "You are an American. Come to us." I found my text: "Have we not all one Father, and is not that God the God of Israel?" It had been the sad lot of the Jews, I pointed out, to be arrayed from earliest times one against the other, and the problem of the Jew anywhere had always been the problem of the Jew everywhere.

One could see that here were women who had grown old and gray through the past years of suffering, and yet had determined that as long as life lasted, they must carry on.

When I returned to America I reported, of course, the great need for the Council to organize a unit, and the Reconstruction Committee immediately sent women throughout the country to raise funds.

In the autumn of 1920 the first unit was despatched with Celia Strakosch at its head. Mrs. Strakosch was a typical American, a graduate of the University of California and director of the Emanu-El Sisterhood. A second unit went over in the spring of 1922 with Mrs. Elinor Sachs-Barr and Doris Maddow at its head. Mrs. Sachs-Barr was a Phi Beta Kappa graduate of Barnard College, with an enviable record as a research worker, and Doris Maddow was also a Barnard College graduate. And in the spring of 1923 a third unit sailed with Clara Greenhut and Dr. Margaret Paukner at the head. Clara Greenhut was a fine example of a daughter from a wealthy Jewish home of New York City, formerly a pupil of mine, and a model of the serious volunteer social worker that is found so often in our best American life. Dr. Paukner was a graduate of a European university and a remarkable linguist, having command of five or six languages. She worked as a representative of both the Joint Distribution Committee and the Council of Jewish Women among the orphans in Poland.

I myself travelled through Europe several times in connection with this work, and in America among the women without whom the work could not have proceeded were Mrs. Henry Moskowitz and Mrs. Clarence Mack.

Once when I was in Berlin I was greatly heartened by the sympathy of one of our fine American Jewesses, Mrs. Henry Morgenthau, who gave me a large sum for our work. She was particularly interested in the needs of the children and also the intellectual classes among the Jews. Much could be said about Mrs. Morgenthau's bounties.

The Jewish women of Rotterdam had requested formally that a unit of workers be sent them, and I recommended that the proposed experiment in social organization be tried there first. I also recommended that the waiting time of the transmigrants at the Montefiore Home be used in learning to read and write English, and that the work be systematized in the place so that all could apply themselves usefully. Almost the last injunction given the departing unit was that a garment repair and cleaning shop be opened, so that the women could mend the clothing of their men. They could also be taught to make garments for their children. The men were to keep the place clean, cut down the weeds in the garden and plow the soil, so that it might be ready for next season's planting.

The Montefiore became a different place after the unit arrived. They carried through successfully all the recommendations, perked up the morale of the refugees, and gave the women of Rotterdam and The Hague demonstrations that moved them to amazement and admiration.

One of the men was encouraged to open a barber shop. All the women received lessons in sanitation; they were taught how to keep clean if only a thimbleful of water was at their disposal. So impressed were the officials of the Holland-America Line that they gave the unit permission to extend its social work to the company's barracks, where emigrants were segregated for disinfecting prior to embarkation. Previously these barracks had been barred to all visitors. The unit was anxious to serve there, as the period of segregation was so wracking and depressing that the benefit of the weeks at the Montefiore was often lost. With the good influence extended up to the very hour of embarkation, it could be felt that immigrants were given a fair start on the way to America. The lessons in English drew large classes, and were of incalculable value in the instilling of Americanism. Even American history was taught.

The following July, about six months after the unit arrived in Holland, a pageant was staged among the inmates of the Montefiore Home. Uncle Sam led the parade, with the American flag. Two children dressed in red, white and blue followed him beating drums. Priscilla Alden, Betsy Ross, George Washington, and other American historical personages were represented.

Among the visitors was a gentleman who had been told of the work at the Montefiore Home, and had heard from Holland-America officials that a Fourth of July celebration was going on. He stood at the edge of the crowd, and as he saw these people already imbued with the spirit of America, tears started from his eyes. It was none other than the United States Commissioner of Immigration, J. Kennedy Todd. Mr. Todd was thoroughly pleased, and agreed with the idea that every moment of time between the decision of an immigrant to go to America and his landing there should be used for his education as an American citizen, and for instilling into him a love and enthusiasm for the land of his adoption. It seemed

Overseas Activities

the American vocabulary of social service were old and well-tried in the European welfare system. True, in several countries the Jewish women were so backward that we represented the latest word in progress. And in all countries we were an important factor because of our freshness and energy and eagerness to be of service. The women of Europe were spent and tired.

Back of us was the energy of the Committee on Reconstruction at home, appointed by the President, Rose Brenner, among whom were Florina Lasker, Mrs. Saml. Rosensohn, Mrs. Irving Lehman, Mrs. Wm. Sporborg, Mrs. Julius Rosenwald.

Among the delegates were physicians, lawyers, two members of the House of Deputies, social workers, paid and volunteer, and the heads of the Zionist groups of Germany, Poland, Roumania, the Ukraine, and elsewhere. To nearly all the delegates the expense of the journey was not only a financial burden but a great physical strain. Yet the cause was worth it. It was not a verbal truce, not a parley beneath which lay vengefulness; it was a gathering of Jewish sisters, who came with peace in their hearts.

The opening of the session was arranged by the women's committee of Vienna, among which was represented the oldest Jewish women's organization in two continents, the Israelitischer Frauenverein, was held at the Rittersaal of the Koenigliche Hofburg, the palace of the former Emperor or Austria. It was addressed by the

President of the Austrian Republic, Dr. Michael Hainisch, and his illustrious mother, Frau Maria Hainisch, the eighty-three-year-old leader of the women of Europe in the struggle for equal rights. Addresses were also made by the Burgomaster of Vienna and other public officials, and by Dr. Chajes, the chief rabbi.

The newspapers of Europe were tremendously interested, the anti-Semitic press of Vienna ceasing its malignant activities for a time and reporting the sessions impartially, without distortion.

At the first working session I was elected President with the following executive committee: Mrs. Gertrude Spielman, England; Fräulein Bertha Pappenheim, Germany; Mrs. Estelle M. Sternberger, U. S. A.; Mrs. Nathaniel Harris, U. S. A.; Mrs. Eichholz, daughter of the former chief rabbi of Great Britain; Mme. Zadoc Kahn, France; Miss van Gelder, Holland; Mrs. Marie Fishman, Latvia, a graduate of the University of Edinburgh, a charming woman and the daughter of wealthy Russian Jews exiled by the Soviet government; Mrs. Klotz, Poland; Mrs. Sachs-Barr, U. S. A.; Frau Anitta Müller-Cohn, Austria.

The fact that an American was chosen President of the Congress was entirely attributable to the feeling of gratitude to the Jews of America for the help and moral support they had given their brothers and sisters in Europe.

I wonder whether many conventions assembled

Overseas Activities

so many striking and interesting personalities. For one thing, I was interested in the fact that there were no less than eleven wives or daughters of rabbis like myself. The European woman with whom I was on closest terms of intimacy, I suppose, was Fräulein Bertha Pappenheim, with whom I still keep up a friendship. She, a wealthy Jewish heiress, was in the vanguard of the women of Germany in doing social work. Thirty years ago she organized the Deutscher Frauenbund, the German equivalent of the Council of Jewish Women. At the Congress she was still so imbued with the spirit of sacrifice that she refused to eat an orange, feeling she had no right to enjoy luxuries while the people went hungry. Nevertheless, the night before the closing of the Congress she, along with the other of the ninety-two delegates, accepted an invitation to attend a gala performance of the opera. And after the opera was over when we all assembled in the grand foyer, she and Dr. Sophie Werner, professor at the University of Hamburg, and Paula Ollendorf, a lecturer and official interpreter of the Congress (she spoke six languages fluently) came to me with tears in their eyes and said that it was the first time in seven years that they had attended a theatrical performance.

One of the most picturesque figures at the Congress was Nannie Margolies, one of the German delegates. She, too, was a university woman, young and very beautiful, one of the most remarkable impromptu speakers I have ever heard. Her outstanding quality was her tremendous passion for the cause of Jewish nationalism.

And speaking of nationalism, or Zionism, I might mention Nellie Straus Moschessohn. This frail, little American woman, a graduate of the New York School of the Ethical Culture Society, had transplanted herself to Palestine and was chosen by the Jewish women of that country to be their delegate to the Congress.

The program of the Congress covered the fields of religion, religious education, child welfare, sex hygiene, and immigration, especially the social care of migrants.

It is well to say, as Dr. Chajes stated, that only after a decade has passed can the full meaning of the Congress be understood and appreciated; that it was epoch-making in its importance, and has given to the Jewish women of Europe a new outlook on social problems. It has also given the Council of Jewish Women of America a new meaning and a new import.

The result of the five days of conference, the spirit of willingness not only to take but to give, and the fine feeling of consideration for the opinions of those with whom one did not and could not agree, gave an exalted tone to Jewish welfare work. One left the Congress feeling that here had been a spiritual gain for the Jews the world over.

Chapter xviii

MY PORTION

DOES it seem so only to me, or has my life been singularly rich in experience? Am I a romanticist? Would another person have found the same life commonplace enough? As I turn the leaves of the past, I find myself growing as interested as though someone in a book, not myself, were the active participant.

For one thing, I think of the twenty-three trips that I made to Europe and marvel at what each has held—those taken on account of George, those for the Council units, and those for mere recreation.

Actually recreation.

The reader who has followed me to this point must think me, I feel, rather a prig who lived and worked simply by a set of sentimental notions in her head. Let the happy care-free times when I and my friends travelled together in Europe speak for my sanity.

One of the most interesting and instructive trips (here sounds the prig again) was the one in which I accompanied Dr. Henry Leipziger and his sister. Dr. Leipziger was distinguished as the founder of the system of free evening lectures in the public schools of New York. He and I became friends not long after Alexander Kohut's death, at the period when I had to earn money in any way possible. He gave me an opening as substitute in the evening lecture department of the schools.

His was an unusually striking personality. Deep-set, glowing eyes above a heavy beard (worn to hide the hollows in his cheeks, the ravages of tuberculosis) gave him the appearance of a fanatic. So did his eager manner, his burning zeal. On or off the lecture platform, this educationalist and lay preacher could hold an audience of a circle of friends spell-bound.

Though his ill health often made him irritable, it was a delight to have a man of his culture and knowledge as a travelling companion. Europe became peopled for me by the shades of the historic figures that he evoked from the past. At the Prison of Chillon, for instance, as we stood looking down into the famous dungeon, he recited the whole of Byron's poem in the resonant voice for which he was celebrated.

On another trip one of the pleasantest incidents I recall was in Rome exchanging reminiscences about Richmond with Sir Moses Ezekiel. There was the renowned sculptor who had fought as a boy in the Confederate army, and had risen to the rank of lieutenant, had been knighted by the king of Italy, had renovated and restored a part of the baths of Diocletian for his studio, which had become one of the show places of the city and was famed for its brilliant gatherings of writers, painters, nobles, diplomats within its tapestried walls—here was this man, eminent, honored, surrounded by magnificence asking me questions about the friends and humble surroundings of his boyhood. Were any of the Michelbacher family still living? Had I any direct news or seen lately any of his relatives, especially his sister, Mrs. Esther Samuels? Did I know that a replica of the statue of George Washington in the Capitol Square in Richmond had been placed in Munich? His most eager longings centered on the little Jewish cemetery with the remarkable railings on Shockoe Hill.

Sir Moses died in 1917, without ever seeing Richmond again, though his body was brought to the United States for burial. His funeral was made a State ceremony, soldiers and sailors firing salutes for a hero as his body was interred in the Arlington National Cemetery, near his own well-known Memorial Group.

Another acquaintance of mine from early days, David Lubin, a fellow-Californian and fellow-Jew who later distinguished himself as the founder of the International Institute of Agriculture, also made Rome his place of residence.

On one of my first visits to Europe I had met Baron and Baroness De Hirsch, the philanthropists who did so much for their co-religionists in all parts of the world. A few years later I enjoyed another visit to Baroness De Hirsch in her home in the Avenue du Bois, Paris. This beautiful woman dressed in simple black, without a jewel on her person, astonished me by her knowledge of all subjects connected with her late husband's philanthropies. When I spoke of the Council of Jewish Women and the Emanu-El Sisterhood, she told me that since their organization she had been following their work through American Jewish periodicals. She wished that French women could be as public-spirited or as generously inclined as their American sisters. Naturally, she was eager to know my opinion of the Clara De Hirsch Home in New York, and expressed regret that it had not prevailed in its purpose of encouraging Jewish girls to enter domestic service.

She asked me to accept a check for the Emanu-El Sisterhood, apologizing that it was not a large sum, merely an expression of appreciation of the Sisterhood's work. She would have liked to devote a large sum to our work, but the greater part of her income was tied up in financing institutions created by her husband.

Once while my daughters and I were in Berlin, we made good use of our time by taking courses. I attended the university as an auditor, and the girls went to school. My interest in the labor movement in America dates from that stay in Berlin.

My Portion 289

At the University one of the professors announced a series of lectures on labor conditions in the United States. This was a subject in which I had had little interest while in New York, but the thought of learning more about my own country while in a foreign land appealed to me by its very incongruity. I attended all the lectures, and found them among the most profitable investments in enlightenment I ever made. The professor was giving these lectures to German students, and it was inevitable that he should stress the differences between American and German labor. Thus I also learned about German labor while familiarizing myself with industrial conditions of my own country. These parallel studies proved fascinating. I learned about the guilds and the progress of the co-operative movement, and even did some research work of my own. The German employment system, in particular, aroused my interest and wonder. Thirty years ago it was already highly developed in Germany, the various bureaus being under government control.

When I returned to the United States I looked upon the industrial world with opened eyes. It seems almost paradoxical that an American who gave most of her time and energy in later years to the development of employment bureaus, and who took a sympathetic interest in the progress of strikes to win better working conditions, should have received her first impetus in Germany.

We made many personal friends there. Several

of them are still alive and are counted among the dearest of those whom we call friends, though the Great War put our friendship to a severe test. It is my feeling that without compromise of principle people who differ politically can yet retain each other's love and respect.

Two friends whom I especially valued were Nahida Remy, celebrated German authoress, and her husband, Professor Moritz Lazarus, who laid the foundations for the study of national psychology. Nahida Remy was a Christian who espoused Judaism upon her marriage. I met them first when visiting Europe with my husband, and again, several years later, at the home of the Steinschneiders, and a third time in Meran, to which they retired for the last days of their lives. It is interesting that I should have known the pioneer psychologist so well, and that a decade later, in America, I should have taken courses under Professor G. Stanley Hall, who brought the study of psychology to this country from Germany and was its pioneer expounder here. Few have equalled Dr. Hall in intellectual stature, in courage, in kindness and tolerance, and in executive ability. I feel that his work as president of Clark University was one of the signal achievements of American education.

Two of my European trips were taken in the company of Seraphine Pisko. Thirty years ago I met her at one of the first open Council meetings. What drew us together, I believe, was that she

My Portion

had also just lost her husband. She came up and introduced herself to me. It was a case of friendship at first sight. And yet when she suggested accompanying me on my European travels—it was the second year of the Kohut School for Girls—I confess my heart sank. Suppose she and I had different ways, suppose we didn't care so much for each other on more intimate acquaintance?

We were hardly out a day when I knew our friendship would stand the test of close association. I knew we should hit it off. For one thing, Seraphine Pisko has a keen sense of humor. And I have never met anyone with a finer sense of justice.

And then there is Dr. Leopold Stieglitz, my friend and family physician, whom I love to call "Dr. Lavender," because he reminds me of Margaret Deland's beautiful character in *Old Chester Tales*.

Altogether, I feel my life has been rich in friendships, some dating back to the old Richmond days, as with Mr. Moses Stroock for one, whose family had been intimates of my father. He has risen to be a prominent lawyer in New York and is active on the Council of the College of the City of New York.

The deep friendships of later years, after a goodly number of mileposts and crossroads have been passed and understanding and discernment have been reached, have come to me also. Of such a sort is mine with Seraphine Pisko. The friends of one's childhood, it is true, have the glamour with which one surrounds everything connected with one's early years; but we are not ready for the abiding relationships until we have matured.

In more recent years there is Dr. Chajes, whom I met for the first time in Vienna when I was working for the Council unit. Almost the first thing a Jew in Vienna said to you was: "Have you met our chief rabbi?" Dr. Chajes walked among his flock with a blessing. He regarded the world as his flock. He gathered in the little children and pleaded for them the world over. I had known two rabbis, my father and my husband, who were my ideals, representing certain fundamental qualities which I have always felt a minister of God should possess. It became my privilege through the war to learn to know another. If it had not been for him and his mediation, the Jews of Austria would have fared worse than those in Poland. Day and night he labored, not only for the poor, that they might live, but for the well-to-do, that they might be spared political intrigue and persecution. He travelled from one end of Europe to another in the cause of his co-religionists, and his co-operation with the Joint Distribution Committee aided its work considerably in Central Europe.

When the University of Vienna and the Seminary were about to close, Dr. Chajes determined that Jewish learning should be kept alive. He

My Portion

formed classes and taught them from five to nine every morning, these being the only hours he could spare from his manifold duties. He collected enough money to provide the professors' maintenance, and thus saved the cause of education. He is the living Johanan ben Zakkai, who has carried himself, as it were, in a coffin, in order that the schools in Israel shall not perish. A young man, he seems old and careworn because of the service he has rendered his people. God has always sent His messengers to Israel in time of need and has spoken through them. Truly Chief Rabbi Chajes is a heaven-sent messenger.

There have been many more friends, people between whom and me more than the mere bond of acquaintanceship has been tied. Yes, my life has been rich in friendships.

But I have tasted the bitterness of disloyalty.

One friend was faithless to what to me was a consecrated fellowship. Ever since I have been warier in my human relationships.

Physical illness, too, has been my lot. For years my abundant energy has carried me through all the drains that work and worry had made upon it. In Europe, serving the cause of the Council unit, the horrible conditions I found among suffering humanity, especially the Jews fleeing from massacre, told upon my health. One day I staggered into the American Hospital in Paris and lay there at death's door from what they called nervous prostration. Soon, however, I was well enough to return to the hotel conducted by the Young Women's Christian Association.

The next trip on behalf of the Unit I had again to go to the American Hospital, and left it after a short time to sail to New York. I am sure that it was the desire to carry on the work in Europe which made it possible for me to walk down the gang-plank instead of being carried on a stretcher.

I have never been really well again.

And so, when I look back and ask myself what has been my portion, it seems miraculously compounded of all the ingredients of life—poverty, struggle, affluence, health, illness, companionship, friendship, love, betrayal, loneliness, giving, taking, doing. For a moment I stop there and say: "That's all. That has been my portion."

But no, life holds even more, and in that more it has been my portion to share, too. Life, above all, is a going on, a never resting. And I see myself always going on, never pausing in the present, always restless, always straining forward for something that has not been but should be.

THE END

INDEX

l'Abbé Constantin, 144
Addams, Jane, 117
Adler, Chief Rabbi, 142
Adler, Felix, 68, 134
Adler, Dr. Herman, 136
Adler, Dr. Isaac, 134, 168, 192, 193, 231
Aguilar, Grace, 72
Akiba, Rabbi, 127
Alexander Kohut Foundations, 241
Alexander Kohut Memorial Collection, 241
Alexander Kohut Memorial Publication Fund, 242
Alexander Kohut Research Fellowship in Semitics, 242
American Hebrew, The, 78, 84, 172, 176
American Hospital, The, in Paris, 293
American Israelite, The, 84
American Jewish Relief Committee, 244, 263, 265
American, Sadie, 182, 200
Anthony, Susan B., 73, 117, 214
Argonaut, The, 41
Apponyi, Miss, 42
Arlington Memorial, 27
Arlington National Cemetery, 287
Aruch Completum, 79, 92, 93, 116, 124, 126, 127, 134, 135, 137, 138, 143-45, 154, 160-65, 180, 241
Ascarelli, Deborah, 72
Ascoli, 164
Avery, Rachel Foster, 209

Babcocks, 240
Bacher, 152

Baldwin Theatre Stock Company, 56
Baltimore, 20, 90, 99, 164
Barbary Coast, 39, 142
Barnard College, 273
Barrett, Lawrence, 75
Barth, 164
Beecher, Henry Ward, 75
Beekman Place, 98, 116, 121, 122, 123, 124, 130, 132, 154, 161, 166, 243
Beer, Mrs. Julius, 203
Belasco, David, 56
Benjamin, Judah P., 27
Berlin, 216, 226, 268, 274
  University of, 229, 288, 289
Berliner Zeitung, 159
Beth Ahabah, Congregation, 14, 17
Beth-El Temple, 83
Bethlen, Count, 4-5
Bettelheim, 55, 80, 253
Bettelheim, Albert Siegfried, 7, 14-15, 171, 172
Bettelheim, Cyd, 112, 255-257
Bettelheim, Esther, 35, 198
Bettelheim, Eva, 7, 257
Bettelheim, Felix, 23, 47-48, 74, 89, 91, 95, 98, 106, 107, 152, 167, 168, 169
Bettelheim, Leopold, 5
Bettelheim, Minnie, 10, 53
Bettelheim, Paul, 91
Bettelheim, Philipp, 146
Bismarck, 159
Bizet, Georges, 144
Blackwell's Island, 123
Blaustein, David, 246
Booth, Edwin, 75
Borg, Mrs. Celia, 238

Index

Brady, Nicholas, Mrs., 264
Brann, 152
Breslau Seminary, 115, 159
Brown University, 246
Brüll, 164
Buber, 164
Budapest, 11, 268
Budapest, Congress of, 79
Buechner, 80

California, University of, 47, 65, 70, 272
Calvary Baptist Church, 156
Calvary, S., 160
Cardinal's Snuff Box, The, 122
Carmen, 144
Castle Garden, 176
Central-and-Southern Pacific Railroad, 87
Central Synagogue, Sisterhood of the, 173
Chajes, Dr., 282, 284, 291, 292, 293
Chancellorsville, 29
Children's Hour, The, 179
Chillon, Prison of, 286
Chinatown, 39, 58
Chronicle, The, 41
Church of the Holy Communion, 250
City of Paris, steamship, 135
Clara De Hirsch Home, 288
Cleveland, Mrs. Grover, 209, 211, 213
Cliff House, 42
Cole, Judge, 122
Colima, The, steamship, 74, 89
Collyer, Robert, 125
Colomans, 11
Columbia University, 155, 208, 229, 237
Columbia University Library, 195
Columbus, Christopher, 148-149
Confederate army, 286
Congress of Mothers, 211
Congress of Religions, 180, 279
Consumers' League, 201, 249
Corvinuses, 11

Council of Jewish Women, 177, 214, 221, 243, 244, 245, 252, 254, 255, 258, 264, 265, 280, 281, 284, 288
Count of Monte Christo, 57
Crown Street Synagogue, 12-13
Cultus-Ministerium, 138
Czernowitz, 9-10

Darwin, Charles, 80
Davis, Jefferson, 27
Davison, Mrs. Henry P., 264
Day, Colonel, 31-32
De Hirsch, Baron, 136, 287
De Hirsch, Baroness, 287, 288
Deland, Margaret, 291
De Lesseps, 74, 91, 167
Delitzsch, Professor Franz, 163
Derenbourg, Professor Joseph, 143
Deutsch, Gotthard, 184
Deutscher Frauenbund, 272, 283
Diocletian, Battles of, 287
Dodge, Grace, 243, 249-252, 255
Dreamers of the Ghetto, 226

Early Babylonian Letters from Larsa, 242
Eaton, Dr. Charles, 125, 156
Educational Alliance, 245, 246, 250, 255
Ehrlich, Professor Arnold B., 125, 177
Eichholz, Mrs., 282
Einhorn, David, 77
Einstein, Mrs. Hannah B., 201, 202, 262
Elba, steamship, 128
Elberfeld, 272
Ely, Miss, 216
Ely School, 214
Elzas, Barnett A., 79
Emanu-El Sisterhood, 173, 202, 237, 238, 255, 262, 273, 288
Honorary President of, 255
Emanu-El Temple, 85, 100, 201, 203, 222, 223, 226
Emanu-El Theological School, 208

Emerson, Ralph Waldo, 110, 180
Ersch and Gruber Encyclopedia, 151
Ethical Culture Society, New York School of the, 284
Ethics of the Fathers, The, 156
Ezekiel, Sir Moses, 27, 286, 287

Fanto's Printing Shop, 144, 145
Federation of Jewish Philanthropic Societies, 266
Federation of Temple Sisterhoods, 253
Fels, Joseph, 18
Fels, Samuel, 18
Felsenthal, Dr. Bernhard, 77, 101
First Baltimore Hebrew Congregation, 111
Fishman, Mrs. Marie, 282
Forgacs, Count, 9
Francesca Da Rimini, 75
Francis Joseph, Emperor, 145
Frankel, 115, 159
Franko, Nahan, 122
Franko, Sam, 122
Freedman, Mrs. Isabella, 202, 262
Freystadt, 10
Frou-Frou, 144
Fruit and Flower Mission, 66-68, 173, 234

Gaillard, Dr., 122
Gaillard, Edwin, and brother, 130
Gamaliel, 127
Gaster, Moses, 142
Genizah, 185
Gerster, Etelka, 10
Gibbons, Cardinal, 19, 108, 111
Gilman, Dr., 111
Gitterman, Dinah, 201
Glay, Professor A. T., 242
Gluck, Alma, 258
Goethals, 167
Goethe, 110
Goldziher, 152
Gorgas, 167
Gottheil, Dr. Gustav, 85, 101, 161, 165, 173, 174, 185, 186, 197, 203, 208, 210, 231, 237, 244

Gottheil, Richard, 244
Graetz, Heinrich, 115, 138, 152, 159, 164, 189
Gramm, Marie, 122
Grant, General, 52
Gratz, Rebecca, 72
Greenhut, Mrs. Clara, 273
Grice, Ettalene N., 243
Grosswardein, 92
Guard, Rev. Dr., 43
Guard, William J., 43
Güdemann, Chief Rabbi, 127, 145
Guggenheim, Mrs. Daniel, 262
Gumpertz-Tellheim, Caroline, 11, 145

Hainisch, Frau Maria, 282
Hainisch, Dr. Michael, 282
Hale, Edward Everett, 180
Halévy, Ludovic, daughter of, 144
Hall, Professor G. Stanley, 290
Hamburg, University of, 283
Hamlet, 75
Hapsburg, Leopold, 11
Harland, Henry, 98, 122
Harland, Justice, 122
Harriman, E. H., 185
Harris, Rev. Maurice H., 245
Harris, Mrs. Nathaniel, 282
Harte, Bret, 60
Harvard University, 179
Hawthorne, Nathaniel, 180
Hearst, Mrs. Phoebe, 65, 209, 211, 213
Hebrew Free School, 175
Hebrew Technical School for Girls, 175, 201
Hebrew Union College, 77, 85, 114, 208
Heilprin, Michael, 125, 176
Heine, 110, 215, 248
Helpful Thoughts, 244
Hertz, Joseph H., Chief Rabbi, 184, 189
Herzl, Dr. Theodor, 218-221
Hilfsverein, 270
Hillel, 127

Index

Hirsch, Emil G., 77, 182, 184
History of the Jews, 189
History of the Jews of Richmond, 14
Hobart, Clario, 63, 64
Hodge, 7
Holland, 268
Hollywood Cemetery, 21
Hooker, 29
House of the Seven Gables, 59
Howe, Julia Ward, 73
Huebsch, Adolph, 92
Hungarian Academy of Science, Royal, 138
Hunt, Caroline Lora, 58, 60, 64, 180
Huntington, Collis P., 87

Il Trovatore, 75
Imber, Naphthali Herz, 125
Immigration, U. S. Commissioner of, 276
Imperial Academy of Science, 138
International Institute of Agriculture, 287
Isaacs, Isaac, 174
Isaacs, Rev. M. S., 174
Isaacs, Minnie, 201
Isaacs, Judge Myer S., 201
Iseman, Marx, 15
Israelitischer Frauenverein, 281
Italy, King of, 287
Ivanhoe, 72

Jackson, Helen Hunt, 60
Jackson, Stonewall, 29
Jacobs, Joseph, 142
Jasper, John, 21-22
Jastrow, Marcus, 76, 80
Jellinek, Dr., 145
Jewett, Fidelia, 71
Jewish Board of Ministers, 203, 204
Jewish Messenger, 174, 176, 201
Jewish Publication Society of America, 115, 189
Jewish Theological Seminary, 85, 114, 115, 139, 157, 184, 208, 239
Jewish Welfare Board, 266
Johns Hopkins University, 110, 111
Joint Distribution Committee, 263, 265, 267, 270, 274, 292
Joseph II, 11

Kahn, Julius, 56
Kahn, Zadoc, Chief Rabbi, 143
Kahn, Mme. Zadoc, 282
Karpeles, Gustav, 153
Kaschau, 10, 12
Kattowitz, 268, 271
Kaufmann, 152
Kautzsch, 164
Kearney, Dennis, 51
Kecskemét, 146-151
  bishop of, 152
Kincaid, Mary, 65, 66, 89, 209, 211, 213
Klotz, Mrs., 282
Kohler, Dr. Kaufmann, 77, 83, 93, 101, 204
Kohut, Adolph, 158, 159
Kohut, Alexander, 12, 78 *et seq.,* 90, 142, 143, 149, 232, 240, 241, 252, 286
  mother of, 146, 148
Kohut, Elizabeth, 103
Kohut, Elsie, 231
Kohut, Eugene, 103
Kohut, George, 103, 162, 183, 189, 190, 194, 207, 208, 216, 226, 227, 229, 231, 236, 239, 240, 242, 285
Kohut, Gisela, 103, 157, 161
Kohut, Helen, 103, 162
Kohut, Louis, 103
Kohut, Margaret, 103, 231
Kohut, Valerie, 103, 163, 231
Kohut School for Girls, 226, 231, 291
Königliche Bibliothek, 217
Komorn, 8-10, 12
Kossuth, Louis, 11, 79, 86, 190
Ku Klux Klan, 20, 53

Index

Ladislauses, 11
Lake poets, 188
Lazarus, Emma, 72, 176, 177, 201
Lazarus, Josephine, 177, 201
Lazarus, Professor Moritz, 290
Lazarus, Sarah, 177
Lee, General, 29
Leeser, Isaac, 13-14
Leipziger, Dr. Henry, 226, 285, 286
Lessing, 110
Leventritt, Mrs. David L., 201
Lilienthal, Dr. Max, 77
Lincoln, Abraham, 43, 117
Linden Hill Cemetery, 190
Liszt, 150, 151
Loew, Reb, 151
Loewe, Dr., 136
London Jewish Chronicle, 142
Longfellow, Henry Wadsworth, 179
Louis, Minnie D., 199, 200
Louis, Minnie D., Downtown Sabbath School, 175
Low, Seth, 155, 249, 251
Lowell, Mrs. Josephine Shaw, 249
Lubin, David, 287
Luckstone, Isidore, 122
Luska, Sidney, 98, 122
Lutz, Dr. F. H., 242
Lyell, 80
Lyons, Sarah, 177, 201

MacArthur, Dr. S. S., 125, 156
Mack, Mrs. Clarence, 274
Maddow, Doris, 273
Maimonides College, 13-14
Man Without a Country, The, 179
Man With The Marble Heart, The, 54
Marbury, Elizabeth, 124
Margolies, Nannie, 283
Marshall, John, 21
Marshall, Louis, 157
Mazzini, 86
Mechanic Pavilion, 52

Memoir of Alexander Kohut, A, 79
Mendelssohn, 72
Mendes, Rev. Dr. H. Pereira, 80, 177, 203
Meran, 226, 290
Metropolitan Opera House, 43
Mexico City, 90
Michelbacher, Rev. Dr. M. J., 17, 287
Millhiser, Moses, 17, 158
Moleschott, 80
Mommsen, 217
Montefiore, Claude, 138, 139
Montefiore, Sir Moses, 136, 137
Montefiore Home, in Rotterdam, 268, 269, 274-276
Morais, Dr. Sabato, 80, 85, 115, 139, 184
Morgan, Anne, 124, 262, 263
Morgenthau, Mrs. Henry, 262, 274
Morse, Salmi, 57
Moschessohn, Nellie Strauss, 284
Moskowitz, Mrs. Henry, 274
Mothers' Congress, 209
"Mount Parnassus," 42
Müller, Professor Friedrich, 163
Müller, Max, 138, 142
Müller-Cohn, Frau Anitta, 271, 282
Myers, Asher, 142
Myers, Gustavus, 27
Myers, Major William B., 27

Nathan, Mrs. Frederick, 201
National Council of Jewish Women, 184, 199
National Geographic Magazine, 135
National Jewish Hospital for Consumptives, 221
Secretary of, 221
National League for Women's Service, 263
Neubauer, Dr. Adolph, 136, 142
New York, 221, 223, 225

300   Index

New York Council, 206, 207
New York University, 230

Old Chester Tales, 291
Ollendorf, Paula, 283
O'Neill, Eugene, 57
O'Neill, James, 57
Orchard Street, House on, 255-258
Osler, William, 169
Othello, 75
Other Things Being Equal, 60
Outre Mer, 180

Pacific Mail Company, 40
Panama, 74, 89, 90, 152
Pappenheim, Bertha, 272, 282, 283
Passion Play, 57
Paukner, Dr. Margaret, 274
People of the Book, The, 245
Philadelphia, 12-13, 110
Pickford, Mary, 117
Pisko, Seraphine, 221, 290
Pittsburgh Conference, 84, 85, 114
Playground Association, 129
Police Gazette, 30-31
Posnanski, Dr. Samuel, 216
Prague, 8
  University of, 9
Presburg, 146
  Seminary of, 8
President of Austrian Republic, 281
Princess Sabbath, 215

Rabbi of Bacharach, 215
Radin, Adolph, 125
Ramona, 60
Ramsgate, 136, 137, 143
Rapoport, Solomon Judah Loeb, 8
Rappahannock, 29
Rebecca of Sunnybrook Farm, 70
Reese, Michael, 42
Remy, Nahida, 290
Renan, Ernest, 138, 164
Rice, Henry, 174
Richman, Julia, 200, 226
Richmond, 14, 88, 89, 166, 223, 286

Richmond Dispatch, 15
Rieger, Dr. Paul, 216
Riverdale-on-the-Hudson, 239, 243, 252
Rockefeller, John D., Jr., 264
Rodkinson, Michael, 125
Rollins, Surrogate, 122
Rosenthal, Toby E., 42
Rothschild, Mme., 143
Rotterdam, 268
Ruskay, Esther S., 201

Sachs-Barr, Mrs. Elinor, 273, 282
St. Thomas's Church, 122
Salvini, Tommaso, 75
Samuels, Mrs. Esther, 287
San Francisco, 20, 38, 142, 230
San Francisco Call, The, 41
Sanger, Professor, 57
San Rafael, 61
Saucelito, 61
Savage, Minot J., 156
Schechter, Dr. Solomon, 138-140, 184-185
Schiff, Jacob H., 124, 138, 139, 161, 165, 184, 185, 194, 197, 207, 224, 225, 227, 231, 262, 266, 267
Schiff, Mrs. Jacob H., 197, 206, 226, 243
School of Philanthropy, 237
Schurz, Carl, 176
Schwarenka, Franz Xavier, 123
Scott, Colonel Thomas, 87
Scott, Sir Walter, 72
Sedgwick, 29
Seligman, Professor Edwin R. A., 245
Shammai, 127
Shaw, Rev. Anna Howard, 214
Shepherd, Elliott, 184
Shockoe Hill, 25-26, 287
Silberstein, Solomon, 125
Simpson, Sampson, 157
Singer, Dr. S., 142
Smith, Gertrude Robinson, 262, 263
Smith, Nora, 69

Smolensky, 164
Solomon, Hannah, 182, 199
Spencer, 80
Spielman, Mrs. Gertrude, 282
Spottsylvania Court-House, 29
Stanton, Elizabeth Cady, 73
Steinschneider, Prof. Moritz, 216, 217, 290
Steinschneider, Mrs. Moritz, 216, 217
Sternberger, Mrs. Estelle M., 282
Stieglitz, Dr. Leopold, 291
Stone, Lucy, 73
Stowe, Harriet Beecher, 73
Straight, Mrs. Willard, 263
Strakosch, Mrs. Celia L., 273
Stroock, Moses, 291
Sullam, Sarah Copia, 72
Sulzberger, Judge Mayer, 184, 212
Sutro, Adolph, 42
Swanson, Gloria, 117
Sweet, John, 42
Sycle, Grandma, 22
Szold, Benjamin, 8, 12, 76, 80, 101, 107, 108, 118, 190
Szold, Mrs. Benjamin, 108
Szold, Henrietta, 109, 118
Szold, Rachel, 109

Talmage, Dr. DeWitt, 156
Temesvár, 9
Texas-and-Pacific Railroad, 87
Thorington, 170
Todd, J. Kennedy, 276
Tonkonogy, Jeanne, 258
Trautman, Mrs. Ralph, 132
Tyndall, 80

Uncle Tom's Cabin, 52, 53
Union of American Hebrew Congregations, 43, 77
Union Pacific Railroad, 185
United Hebrew Charities, 174
United War Work, 264

Vacation Association, 261, 262
Van Gelder, Miss, 282

Victoria, Queen, 141, 142
Vienna, Burgomaster of, 282
Vienna, Royal Academy of, 136
Vienna Seminary, 241, 292
Vienna, University of, 292
Virginia Medical College, 18
Vogelstein, Dr. Hermann, 216

Wald, Lillian D., 175
Wales, Prince of, 142
Walker, Mary, 72, 73
Waller's Tavern, 29
Walters, the, 203
Warburg, Felix M., 266
Ward, Dr. William Hayes, 124
Wechsler, Rev. J., 14-15
Werner, Dr. Sophie, 283
Wetmore, Maude, 262, 263
Wiggin, Kate Douglas, 69, 70
Wilson, Mary, 111
Wise, Aaron, 101
Wise, Isaac M., 43-44, 76, 77, 84, 85, 114, 124, 184, 208
Wise, Stephen S., 101, 125, 184, 189, 241
Wolf, Emma, 61
Women's Christian Temperance Union, 215, 216
Women's Health Protective Association, 132, 173, 204
Women's Municipal League, 249
World Congress of Jewish Women, 277, 289, *et seq.*
President of, 282
World's Fair, 180

Yale University, 241, 242
Yemenite Jews, 184, 185
Yoke of the Torah, The, 98, 116, 122
Young Israel, 244
Young Women's Christian Association, 249, 261, 265, 293
Young Women's Hebrew Association, 259-262

Zakkai, Johanan ben, 293
Zangwill, Israel, 142, 226, 248

The Modern Jewish Experience

An Arno Press Collection

Asch, Sholem. **Kiddush Ha-Shem:** An Epic of 1648. 1926

Benjamin, I[srael ben] J[oseph]. **Three Years in America:** 1859-1862. 1956. Two vols. in one.

Berman, Hannah. **Melutovna.** 1913

Besant, Walter. **The Rebel Queen.** 1893

Blaustein, David. **Memoirs of David Blaustein.** 1913

Brandes, George. **Reminiscences of My Childhood and Youth.** 1906

Brinig, Myron. **Singermann.** 1929

Cahan, A[braham]. **The White Terror and the Red.** 1905

Chotzinoff, Samuel. **A Lost Paradise.** 1955

Cohen, Morris Raphael. **A Dreamer's Journey.** 1949

Cowen, Philip. **Memories of an American Jew.** 1932

Cooper, Samuel W. **Think and Thank.** 1890

Davitt, Michael. **Within the Pale.** 1903

Dembitz, Lewis N. **Jewish Services in Synagogue and Home.** 1898

Epstein, Jacob. **Epstein:** An Autobiography. 1955

Ferber, Edna. **Fanny Herself.** 1917

Fineman, Irving. **Hear, Ye Sons.** 1933

Fishberg, Maurice. **The Jews:** A Study of Race and Environment. 1911

Fleg, Edmond. **Why I Am a Jew.** 1945

Franzos, Karl Emil. **The Jews of Barnow.** 1883

Gamoran, Emanuel. **Changing Conceptions in Jewish Education.** 1924

Glass, Montagu. **Potash and Perlmutter.** 1909

Goldmark, Josephine. **Pilgrims of '48.** 1930

Grossman, Leonid Petrovich. **Confession of a Jew.** 1924

Gratz, Rebecca. **Letters of Rebecca Gratz.** 1929

Kelly, Myra. **Little Aliens.** 1910

Klein, A. M. **Poems.** 1944

Kober, Arthur. **Having Wonderful Time.** 1937

Kohut, Rebekah. **My Portion** (An Autobiography). 1925

Leroy-Beaulieu, Anatole. **Israel Among the Nations.** 1904

Levin, Shmarya. **Childhood in Exile.** 1929

Levin, Shmarya. **Youth in Revolt.** 1930

Levin, Shmarya. **The Arena.** 1932

Levy, Esther. **Jewish Cookery Book on Principles of Economy Adapted for Jewish Housekeepers.** 1871

Levy, Harriet Lane. **920 O'Farrell Street.** 1947

Lewisohn, Ludwig. **Mid-Channel.** 1929

Lewisohn, Ludwig. **The Island Within.** 1928

Markens, Isaac. **The Hebrews in America.** 1888

Martens, Frederick H. **Leo Ornstein.** 1918

Meade, Robert Douthat. **Judah P. Benjamin.** 1943

Mendoza, Daniel. **The Memoirs of the Life of Daniel Mendoza.** 1951

Meredith, George. **The Tragic Comedians.** 1922

Nichols, Anne. **Abie's Irish Rose.** 1927

Nordau, Max. **The Conventional Lies of Our Civilization.** 1895

Nyburg, Sidney L. **The Chosen People.** 1917

Pinski, David. **Three Plays.** 1918

Roth, Cecil. **A History of the Marranos.** 1932

Roth, Cecil. **A Life of Menasseh Ben Israel.** 1934

Rubinow, I[saac] M. **Economic Conditions of the Jews in Russia.** 1907

Sabsovich, Katherine. **Adventures in Idealism.** 1922

Sachs, A[braham] S. **Worlds That Passed.** 1928

Seide, Michael. **The Common Thread.** 1944

Steiner, Edward A. **From Alien to Citizen.** 1914

Untermeyer, Louis. **Roast Leviathan.** 1923

Weinstein, Gregory. **The Ardent Eighties.** 1928

Yezierska, Anzia. **Hungry Hearts.** 1920

Yiddish Tales. 1912

Zangwill, Israel. **The Melting-Pot.** 1932

Zunser, Eliakum. **Selected Songs of Eliakum Zunser.** 1928